# A Guide to Teaching Effective Seminars

*A Guide to Teaching Effective Seminars* provides college and university faculty with a new approach to thinking about their teaching and helps them develop a deeper understanding of conversation itself. Seminars often inspire collaborative learning and produce rich educational environments, yet even experienced faculty find these conversations can range in quality. *A Guide to Teaching Effective Seminars* addresses this challenge by presenting a sociolinguistic perspective on seminars and providing instructors with best practices to manage successful seminars. Grounded in research, data, and her own deep experience teaching seminars, author Susan Fiksdal reveals ways students negotiate perspectives on reading, on conversation, and on social identities and power. By giving readers an appreciation of the discourse of seminars, the book helps to undermine stereotypes about language and people, increase civility, reduce misunderstandings, and foster tolerance for new ideas and diverse ways of expressing them. This important resource is for faculty members at all levels of experience and in every discipline who want practical advice about facilitating effective seminars.

Special Features:

- Each chapter explores a key aspect of conversation with examples from a wide range of seminars across disciplines.
- Transcripts from videotaped seminars showcase authentic conversations and negotiations between students.
- End-of-chapter best practices promote critical thinking and collaboration.
- A companion website features video clips of the transcripts in the book and additional resources.

**Susan Fiksdal** is Member of the Faculty in Linguistics and French at The Evergreen State College, USA.

# A Guide to Teaching Effective Seminars

## Conversation, Identity, and Power

Susan Fiksdal

Routledge
Taylor & Francis Group

NEW YORK AND LONDON

First published 2014
by Routledge
711 Third Avenue, New York, NY 10017

and by Routledge
2 Park Square, Milton Park, Abingdon, Oxon OX14 4RN

*Routledge is an imprint of the Taylor & Francis Group, an informa business*

© 2014 Taylor & Francis

*Library of Congress Cataloging in Publication Data*
Fiksdal, Susan.
  A guide to teaching effective seminars: conversation, identity, and
  power/Susan R. Fiksdal.
  pages cm
  Includes bibliographical references and index.
  1. Seminars. 2. College teaching—Cross-cultural studies.
  3. Learning—Cross-cultural studies. I. Title.
  LB2393.5.F55 2014
  378.1'77--dc23
  2013038731

ISBN: 978-0-415-83989-1 (hbk)
ISBN: 978-0-415-83990-7 (pbk)
ISBN: 978-0-203-77067-2 (ebk)

Typeset in Perpetua and Bell Gothic
by Florence Production Ltd, Stoodleigh, Devon, UK

Printed and bound in the United States of America by Publishers Graphics,
LLC on sustainably sourced paper.

# Contents

# Acknowledgments

I want to thank the students, staff, and faculty at The Evergreen State College. Many faculty and students agreed to be videotaped, interviewed, and surveyed, and without their willingness to participate in my research, I could never have written this book. In addition, I have learned a great deal from my colleagues and students over the years about seminar best practices and I hope I've included all of the best ones.

For her encouragement and advice, I want to thank Carolyn Martin Shaw. We exchanged our writing and provided honest critiques when we were living in Hong Kong and after. Others who have generously given their time and comments include Sunshine Campbell, George Freeman, José Gómez, Rachel Hastings, Amy Hitchcock, Mukti Khanna, Toska Olson, Richard Mack, Virginia Mack, Doug Roscoe, Christina Volkmann, and Brian Walter. Sean Williams convinced me I could complete this project in her wonderful workshop called "Write that Book!" For her careful proofreading and advice on clear writing I thank Esmé Ryan. Paul McMillin and Miko Francis gave useful assistance in the Library. And, I owe many thanks to an anonymous reviewer for very useful comments and the innovative way to help readers understand fractions of a second in conversations by listening to the beat of "Stayin Alive."

Students who helped videotape and interview students were Siri Mehus and Phil Roe and their work was central to my second research project. Students who contributed detailed transcripts and careful analyses in the third project were Caroline Hinchliff and Celia Crossett. Carrie Brownstein volunteered to videotape seminars in my third project even though she had graduated, and she provided solid analyses. Four videographers—Kirk Miller, Saro Calewarts, Peter Ivey, and Halle Hennessey—did a great job. Six interviewers—Cathy Clausen, Kevin Kelly, Kimberly Kinchen, Anna Matzinger, Kristen Mehus, and Michael Toma—followed protocol and gave me useful insights from students. And, finally, students in my Art of Conversation classes who interviewed students about seminars also provided useful data for this book.

Early on, media staff at Evergreen, especially Dominique Sepser and Ally Hinkle, were amazing problem-solvers at every level of gathering data. The Assessment Study Group led by Steve Hunter gave me two small grants to complete my manuscripts. Laura Coghlan sent me results of interviews with students her office conducted in Institutional Research. I used sabbaticals and stolen moments to write and research this book over the years. All of my students and teaching partners helped refine my thinking about how to convey sociolinguistic concepts and I am grateful to them. Faculty who attended my workshops on teaching effective seminars helped me recognize problems, refine my thinking, and learn, especially Zahid Sharif, Doranne Crable, and Joe Tougas, who worked with me at times as co-conveners.

My editor, Heather Jarrow, supported my book proposal and has made its publication possible, for which I am very grateful.

My family, especially my husband, Allen, understood my longing to write this book and gave me the space and time to get it done. I thank them for their patience, love, and support.

# Chapter 1

# Introduction

Seminars in a college or university setting are a time for students to learn how to enter conversations that faculty see as important. In most other class activities such as lectures, labs, field trips, rehearsals, critique sessions, and workshops, the faculty member is in charge and there are clear guidelines in place. Seminars, on the other hand, are facilitated by faculty members, not controlled by them, and what happens depends on the level of serious inquiry that students provide. Seminars help students learn how to analyze texts and gain a sense of why they matter. Most importantly, seminars help students develop a voice. Developing a voice begins with getting the floor in seminar. This is not as easy as it seems, as this book will demonstrate. But having a voice in the conversation is more than hearing yourself talk; it has to do with voicing ideas in a public way and gaining confidence in doing that. As I will show, developing a voice both literally and metaphorically needs to be done in collaboration with others in seminar. Students assess, weigh, contrast, and improve ideas, and their voices gain credibility and authority in the group. In this book we will see that this process of gaining a voice is not just an intellectual journey, but a social one that is intricately linked to identity and power.

Seminars are open-ended, loosely structured conversations. In seminars, students and the faculty member sit together in a circle and discuss topics students have generated after reading a text. The faculty member or a designated student facilitates the conversation. This is quite different from a typical class discussion where the faculty member stands in front of rows of students, asks most of the questions, and manages the talk. By changing the seating arrangement so that students look at each other, they can imagine developing their own conversations. They learn to consider each other as serious contributors to the collaborative learning of the group. This arrangement also makes students' interactions public; everyone can see what everyone else is doing—listening, talking, taking notes, sleeping. If students are sitting in rows, they can more easily remain passive because their personal space is more private. Seminars are a community of practice in which students develop specific ways of speaking—practices that are well understood in academic settings. Learning to teach seminars effectively is crucial because that learning is taking place in a social arena with all the variables we encounter in our everyday lives, especially in the construction of power and identity.

It may seem odd to consider students' power and identity in seminars since the faculty member clearly has great authority. If we consider graduate-level seminars, some will remember with a little twinge some of the issues of power and authority at play for students when they responded to tough questions. The seminar originated in the nineteenth century in German research-based universities. The format was fixed: a student presented an essay that was then critiqued by other students and the professor. The other students would also read on the topic so that they would have an informed discussion (Kruse, 2006). In the United States, this is still largely the format used in humanities and social science graduate courses. In these seminars, the faculty member's authority is clear and the expectation of competition among the students is also clear. In undergraduate seminars, however, a more egalitarian spirit reigns. This egalitarian spirit poses some challenges for faculty members since they need to negotiate their own power and authority as they help students understand theirs. Students may not always have verbal fluency in a discipline, but they have questions, theories, and, most important, a particular perspective on the reading that may be theirs alone.

Hearing multiple perspectives is the most exciting part of seminars. These perspectives come from the students' own lives, from their experience of previous classroom discussions, and their understanding of the disciplinary or interdisciplinary approaches they are learning. For most students, this may be the first time they have heard multiple views on a topic, and the first time that many of these views seem potentially useful or plausible or even confusing. They quickly discover that there is seldom one answer to a question, and that the question itself can be explored in terms of the assumptions it makes. In effective seminars, students discuss good ideas in depth, pay close attention to each other's contributions, help each other by building on ideas, see implications of those ideas, and take notes on what they're learning. Students find connections between the texts they've already studied and themes in the class and learn the difference between analysis and synthesis. They see the relevance of their own ideas to the learning community and the importance of participation because even though there are disagreements, students are sensitive to each other's points of view. But there is much more going on and the stakes are high for everyone involved.

Some quotes from faculty will clarify this:

- *I really think the seminar is critical in helping students gain an intellectual life.*
- *Seminar is such an open question for me—it's never the same sort of experience.*
- *Seminar is essential and hearing your own voice is essential to claim it. You don't take yourself seriously until you hear yourself in public.*

Most of us, faculty members and students alike, have an idealized vision of what we expect to hear in seminar—academic discourse—and that vision is a reasoned, articulate conversation including thoughtful questions where learning is evident in "ah hah" moments. We may believe in this vision even if we have participated in many seminars and the talk has not been completely reasoned, focused, or articulate and learning is not immediately evident. Besides this, it turns out that students often have very divergent assessments of their seminar. One student can be annoyed by tangents, another can find them energizing. I used to ask myself, what is going on?

## SPECIAL FEATURES

As a sociolinguist who studies conversation, I decided to apply my own research in metaphor, gender, and rapport to seminars beginning in the early 1990s. I shared my findings with faculty and students regularly at my college and at other colleges. I also published journal articles. But my colleagues wanted more. This book is my response. It reveals what is going on in seminars by showing how identity and power are intertwined with intellectual inquiry and the building of community.

This book explains the interactions in seminars so you will understand how to help students move to new and deeper levels of analysis. In each chapter, I explain one aspect of the conversation from a linguistic perspective. As I reveal conversational practices, I use examples of student interactions in the form of short transcriptions. To appeal to readers in every discipline, I try to avoid technical terms. For those that have slipped through, I provide a glossary. In the transcriptions, I use symbols to indicate the manner of speaking because pauses, overlaps, word searches, laughter, and voice quality are part of the oral performance. It is possible to read my description of that talk, however, and understand the point I am making even if you don't have the time to decipher the transcriptions. At the end of each chapter, I provide best practices for effective teaching relevant to that chapter. These practices are based on my teaching, colleagues' insights, and research. The website for this book has video clips of many of the transcriptions, and additional resources that illustrate styles of talking and provide further reading. This book is, then, a guide to how students negotiate ideas in seminar and how to facilitate that negotiation effectively.

## APPROACH TO TEACHING SEMINARS

To teach effective seminars there is no map, bag of tricks, or magic. Instead, you need to be flexible and to improvise within the context of your chosen texts and each new group of students. An analogy is to think of yourself as a guest conductor who needs to get to know the musicians quickly. Through practice, you all come to understand the music in new ways as you attune yourselves to the contributions from each musician. Your goals are to help students understand the content and form of the text as well as to build community and teach critical reading and thinking. You are also helping students understand their own thinking processes better to improve and develop their own voice. Because of these multiple goals, your seminars can always be effective. My goal in this book is to help you teach effective seminars.

My central claim is that in seminars, as students choose words to contribute ideas to the conversation, they are constructing and negotiating identities and power in a finely tuned improvisational performance. We construct our social identities by the way we talk, behave, dress, and adorn ourselves. These social identities are not fixed. We all have multiple identities depending on our race, class, gender, age, sexual orientation, ethnicity, geographical region, abilities, nationality, and accent, among other things. Sometimes one of these identities becomes salient. I have heard a student begin to talk about experiences back home, and suddenly I detect an accent that I hadn't noticed before. Sometimes students' identities can be a source of power; for example, they can claim authority about an idea in seminar because they know first-hand what it is like to grow up in a mixed-race neighborhood. As we convey ideas, we also reveal parts of our identities because identities are not fixed or immediately apparent all of the time. Instead, we reveal them as we talk.

Power is also something we perform. Sometimes power relations need to be negotiated when a student is afraid to speak up, others feel silenced, or a group of talkers takes over. Power can come from identity if a particular one is valued. Students may demonstrate that they have grasped an idea, which gives them the floor and the ability to assess other explanations. But the very next moment, if their explanations falter, that power drops away. Besides performing identities and negotiating power, in seminars we are performing in real time, moment by moment. Seminars are part of an orality that we understand from our everyday conversations. We don't have a script, we don't know the outcome, and we don't know who might offer a terrific idea. It is a conversation with lots of voices, so we need to develop ways to know when students want to talk and help them strategically time their entry into the conversation. Directing that performance is our central concern in teaching effective seminars.

Students understand seminar as performance because they know they need to contribute; however, it can be very hard to do that. During seminar everyone is learning more about the text under discussion as well as learning how to conduct an inquiry on an academic topic, so it can be hard to hear what might be going on and misunderstandings can occur. In addition, students hold particular views about seminar, and by looking at metaphors they use to describe the conversation, we can find better ways to help everyone become engaged. As researchers have pointed out, metaphors can inform us about how we think. When we talk about *getting off track* in seminar or *going around in circles*, these metaphors reveal that we conceptualize seminar as a journey. The central values in this metaphor, then, are staying on the path and moving toward a particular destination. In this book I will point out a number of metaphors that each have different organizing principles. Understanding them will help you guide seminars more effectively.

I teach at The Evergreen State College, a public, experimental college that was founded in the late 1960s when a large shift occurred in higher education towards student-centered learning, interdisciplinary classes, egalitarianism, experiential learning, and a focus on teaching (Kliewer, 2001). Because the curriculum at my college is largely structured with full-time (16 credit) interdisciplinary team-taught "programs" that may never repeat, seminar is a time for students to work on their understanding of disciplinary concepts and to make connections between disciplines. Seminars and other forms of student-centered group work are now common in colleges and universities as being central to learning communities. Learning communities are based on improving the social nature of learning, using collaborative structures that place responsibility on students as well as faculty for learning (Laufgraben & Shapiro 2004; Gabelnick et al. 1990). They can be found in freshmen interest groups, linked courses, interdisciplinary programs or courses, and graduate courses. Seminars can focus on any common experience such as a text, performance, film, field experience, or project. Those I discuss here are focused on book seminars.

Seminars are similar to everyday conversations in many ways, but they differ in a crucial respect: the primary goal is to learn more about a text in relationship to a set of concepts and to do that collaboratively in a college classroom. Unlike most informal conversations, the group is generally large—from 20 to 25 students. In addition, there is an expectation of learning complex concepts and terminology drawn from academic disciplines and memories of past seminars and class activities. Seminars take place weekly or bi-weekly in a particular place with an evaluator, the faculty member. There are many similarities between seminars and everyday conversations: humor, false starts, repetitions, long pauses, overlaps and interruptions, people who hold the floor too long, people who don't talk, sudden collective excitement over an idea, disagreements, and misunderstandings. We also witness power plays and identity displays. For example, students can refer to reading or research that no one else is familiar with, making claims and holding forth in an attempt to demonstrate authority and power. Or, they can reveal experiences that have formed their identity, and given them insight into the text. Seminars provide a regularly occurring conversation that can open new ways of thinking, new motivation for learning, new respect for differences, and a new appreciation of others' contributions. As we explore the ways in which students express themselves, readers will begin to understand what's going on more clearly and may also build more tolerance for different ways of interacting in seminars, class discussions, and ordinary conversations outside of the classroom.

As a faculty member who includes seminars in every course, I try to help students learn in seminar by creating their own analysis and synthesis of the material we are examining. This requires helping students develop better critical thinking skills as well as learning to listen to each other. I know from personal experience and from my research that seminars are not always a time for collaborative learning. Sometimes they are uncomfortable and students can be hurt. Faculty members can miss these uncomfortable moments and even if they notice them, they can feel unsure about what to do. That is why I offer best practices from my own experience, from my colleagues, and from other researchers.

## WHO THIS BOOK IS FOR

I have written this book for faculty who want to teach effective seminars, no matter what your discipline or type of course. Because teaching seminars has to do with facilitating the conversation, this book will be useful for student facilitators as well. I believe that translating linguistic discoveries to those outside linguistics is very important. Understanding the practices we use in conversation is essential to good facilitation and good teaching. I have larger goals as well. With more understanding of the conversations we have in seminar and our everyday lives, we can undermine stereotypes about language and people, increase civility, reduce misunderstandings, and foster tolerance for new ideas and diverse ways of expressing them.

You might be wondering why a sociolinguist feels compelled to explain seminars. In all classroom discussions from elementary through higher education, students enter into what has been aptly called a community of practice. The *community* is composed of the students and faculty member for at least one term. The *practice* is learning to approach questions and texts from particular disciplinary or interdisciplinary perspectives and to apply concepts to the reading. Students make connections to personal experience, other readings and material in the class, and to the wider social, political, and economic worlds around them. Some students are new to the practice—they are peripheral learners, observing, and beginning to make contributions. We can help those students, and the more advanced, by understanding that we all draw upon particular linguistic practices that promote or hedge our points, indicate disagreement or agreement, save face, construct social identities, and position other speakers.

## COMMUNITIES OF PRACTICE

The concept of the community of practice was introduced by Jean Lave and Etienne Wenger (1991) who were interested in how people learn. They suggest that learning a craft through apprenticeships can be a useful analogy to many learning situations. Central to this idea is that conversation and observation are ways of learning for many social and cultural groups. Even if formal structures like a classroom exist, learning goes on outside the classroom as well. Learning is a social practice based in particular situations; learning is not only an individual practice. Lave and Wenger point out that learners start with peripheral roles and then become experts. Learning to problem solve, anticipate what will come next, and improvise all lead to expertise. It is important to realize that all members of a community of practice, such as a seminar, are also members of other communities of practice: families, workgroups, bands, dorms, sports teams, clubs, activist groups, etc. In each of these groups, there are ways of greeting, accepted topics of conversation and ways of talking about those topics, and students have developed various levels of expertise in each.

In classrooms from kindergarten through higher education, there are several familiar practices; for example, teachers ask questions, students respond, and the teacher then evaluates that response. This type of questioning is known as initiation-response-feedback (Sinclair & Coulthard, 1975). The questions teachers ask are those whose answers they already know, and the students know that. For that reason, these are called display questions. When students respond, the teacher provides feedback and if the feedback is missing, students can feel hurt or confused because they are so attuned to this structure. In classroom discussions this structure can vary, of course, with other students providing the feedback or initiating topics. The common understanding, however, is that the teacher or faculty member is still the primary evaluator. The display question is often part of lectures at the college level as a way of checking comprehension. It is a teacher-centered approach to talk in the classroom.

Another feature of the talk in classrooms is that pauses between turns can be much longer than in an informal conversation. If teachers pause for 10 seconds or more, they can still hold the floor to think for a while without being interrupted because they are the authority. Students may interact with other students, correcting or encouraging them but the teacher determines the length of these turns and whether or not the topic is appropriate. The teacher also manages the discourse by calling for one speaker at a time if many students are talking at once. It is also important to realize that even in discussions where teachers have a certain degree of authority, students can resist their power by not responding, challenging the agenda, or pretending misunderstanding.

Seminars are part of this community of practice. Each seminar group becomes familiar with each member's conversational practices, intellectual stance, and ways of thinking but this familiarity may not invite careful listening or encouragement. Part of the reason is that in each seminar, as well as each conversation, we are constructing identities, positioning ourselves and others, agreeing and disagreeing, trying not to lose face, using different conversational styles, and improvising our talk moment by moment.

All of our everyday conversations are improvised because they are unplanned. We may be able to introduce a question or a topic we had rehearsed in advance, but it is not always easy. Unlike writing, where we can endlessly revise each sentence in a paragraph, an article, a story, or a lecture, we are not in complete control of our utterances. Instead, we modify and negotiate our talk depending on the other speakers who may understand or misunderstand our ideas and give or reject our right to talk. We cannot even plan how long our conversation might last as this, too, is dependent not just on us. It is often quite difficult to end a conversation at the precise moment we choose.

Besides these features, in all of our conversations we recycle phrases from other conversations, sometimes very directly. You may hear or use phrases such as *that's the way it goes* or *what are you gonna do?* These are fixed phrases that avoid an explicit evaluation. They usually come after a short narrative or story, and either the speaker or listener can use them. These and many other phrases come from other conversations and are, in a sense, borrowed for the occasion. Another way that we do this in conversations is to quote someone else, *She said, Hold on tight! And I just laughed*. We might use pop catchphrases such as *That's so last year* or *That's a no-brainer*. We are creative in our talk, but not always original. In seminars, using common pop catchphrases can be useful in some contexts, but students find they begin to recycle other sorts of phrases—the ones they hear in lectures and read in their texts—they begin to learn academic discourse.

Why is seminar important? Often students believe that seminars are a place to talk and demonstrate their intelligence, and learning to do this is certainly important, but a central outcome of seminar is to learn to really listen—to hear other voices and to value them. Seminars help students develop new world views and to move beyond, often unconscious, biases. As they participate in seminars, students see that working across differences is valuable, and they learn facilitation skills to allow that work. They find that collaboration is valuable and that competition has limitations: pooling knowledge results in more complex reasoning. Students discover the importance of accepting responsibility for their own learning. By coming prepared for seminar, they can learn from others and contribute to everyone's learning. Finally, students learn to cope with ambiguity and paradox—they no longer see problems as merely black and white or believe that questions have just one answer. Seminars, then, prepare students for the workplace and life. In both arenas, they need skills in crucial thinking and careful listening.

## ORGANIZATION OF THE BOOK

In each chapter I explain what is going on in seminar by looking closely at one aspect of the conversations and I provide best practices based on the linguistic patterns I discuss. In Chapter 2, *Moving from Lectures to Seminars*, I introduce seminars to faculty who may be unfamiliar with allowing students the authority to explore ideas in class. I provide a developmental approach I used when I taught a class at a Hong Kong university, where students had been socialized to listen passively to lectures rather than actively participate. I explain how to move smoothly from lectures to seminars in one term, using interactive lectures, workshops, and seminars. In addition, I address important parts of teaching seminars such as choosing the texts and helping students prepare for effective seminars.

In Chapter 3, *Power and Ways of Talking*, I introduce ways of thinking about language that seem uncontroversial, such as using Standard English in class. I critique the assumption that this type of English is the only acceptable language in seminar and introduce the notion of a language ideology that can prevent faculty from hearing ideas offered by students who have nonstandard dialects or speak informally. I show that the ways we talk are part of our identities and this is also a topic in Chapter 4, *Improvisation and Performance: The Importance of Timing*. In this chapter I demonstrate that, like jazz musicians, we are all improvisers in real time. We have conversational styles that can affect how we interact and how others evaluate us. Students may seem to grab power by talking a lot, but they may only be following different cultural norms. Our improvisation relies on an underlying tempo, which is part of a conversational synchrony that is verbal and nonverbal.

Part of entering the conversation has to do with taking a turn, and this can be difficult for students because of the improvisational nature of seminar. In Chapter 5, *Getting the Floor*, I identify six metaphors that reveal how students think about seminar. Some of the metaphors students use include: *getting off on a tangent, building on each other's ideas, engaging in the conversation, throwing out ideas,* and *jumping in*. If students use different metaphors, this can affect how they approach seminar and form their expectations and personal goals.

In Chapter 6, *Performing Identities*, I focus on the ways that students gain authority in seminar by using phrases that indicate the evidence for their ideas. I also discuss ways that faculty members may intend to grant authority to a student by saying, for example, *You're Native American, what do you think?* I show how this labeling actually restricts authority and offends students. On the other hand, students sometimes claim authority by revealing their identities, and this can be effective in getting the floor and developing voice.

Chapter 7, *Agreeing to Disagree* begins with the assumption that we need to agree that we will disagree in seminar—contesting ideas is important in learning to think critically. The focus is on disagreements and how students argue to win or argue to persuade. I show the ways that students maintain and save face for others as they assess each other's contributions and how arguments to win are ineffective and even destructive.

In Chapter 8, *Cross-Cultural Dynamics*, I focus on cultural differences including race, ethnicity, class, gender, sexual orientation, and accent. Some of these differences rise to the surface in seminar and some do not, but social identities nonetheless matter in all of our conversations. Understanding cultural cues, microaggression, and gender dynamics is crucial to students' learning. Because not all classes are face-to-face, Chapter 9, *Electronically Speaking*, focuses on synchronous or online seminars. These forums have some similarities with face-to-face seminars because collaborative learning is the goal, and the issues of identity, power, face, and performance are present even though they are written conversations.

The definition for seminar in the dictionary lists it as a noun; at my college it is a noun, adjective, and a verb. Throughout the book, I often use the word *seminar* without an article in order to emphasize that it is a process and not a thing. As a result, you will see phrases such as *in seminar* and *during seminar*. I emphasize throughout the book that seminars are improvisations in time just like our everyday conversations. With a small turn of phrase, I hope to reflect that fact in my writing.

## CONCLUSION

One of the major reasons I wanted to write this book was to help faculty members create effective seminars that encourage and reward learning and avoid misunderstandings. I believe you can become a better facilitator not by having a grab bag of best practices but a deeper understanding of conversation itself. Also, although ideally seminars should be safe environments, it is a goal that we may not always achieve. Neither students nor faculty members can imagine all of the sorts of comments or situations that could potentially hurt or impact them. I do believe that we can become more aware of what's going on and in that process we will become more tolerant and understanding of the differences we encounter both in seminars and in our lives. Learning to listen to everyone, learning to facilitate the conversation, learning to engage with the ideas—all are worthy goals and all are topics of this book.

## A NOTE ABOUT METHODOLOGY

If you are not a researcher, you may want to skip this section as it provides detail about the data used for this book.

The transcriptions come primarily from four studies I conducted at my college from 1990 to 2013. Three studies involved face-to-face seminars that involved 14—25 students and one faculty member in each. In the first study completed in 1991, I videotaped three seminars in one yearlong interdisciplinary course at two points over the year and invited students and faculty to watch and comment on

## A NOTE ABOUT TRANSCRIPTIONS

The transcriptions I present in this book capture some of the characteristics of the talk. I will use the following conventions:

| | |
|---|---|
| (.) | A brief pause. |
| *Was* | Italics indicate a stressed syllable or word. |
| (2) | A two-second pause. |
| (( )) | Actions the speaker performs are described. |
| [ | The speaker overlaps the previous one at this point. |
| = | The speaker allows no pause after the previous speaker. |
| ↑ | Indicates rising intonation. |
| . | Indicates falling intonation. |
| [. . .] | Indicates omitted talk. |
| – | Indicates a false start. |

20-minute edited versions of the seminar. The playback sessions were audiotaped. I also interviewed 15 randomly selected faculty members about seminar practices. The results were presented in *Seminar Talk*, an unpublished manuscript. In the second study completed in 1993, I and my research assistants videotaped 19 seminars, inviting students and faculty to individually view and comment upon 30-minute edited versions of the seminar. My student assistants also conducted a survey of 64 students about seminar practices. The results were presented in *Getting the Floor*, an unpublished manuscript. For the third study in 2005, my research assistant videotaped 14 seminars and the seminar participants viewed the edited version of their seminar in group settings. I recorded their comments by hand. I also videotaped three of my own seminars in linguistics courses over the years that were not included in these studies. The findings from the unpublished manuscripts and my third study are reported here for the first time. I also present findings from my published work and work by other researchers.

Of 42 videotapes, 30 were analyzed for this book. Others were eliminated due to poor recordings or other technical reasons. All seminars were videotaped with one camera. In each study, students could sit with their backs to the camera if they chose. I asked individual participants whether or not the video camera bothered them and the overwhelming majority said that it did not. My goal was to capture seminars in action, but as William Labov (1972) pointed out, there is an observer's paradox. I wanted to capture naturally occurring talk when it is not observed, yet I could not do that unless I recorded or observed the talk. By taping regularly occurring seminars, which were an integral part of interdisciplinary classes, I hoped that the practices of the learning community and individual goals for learning would outweigh worries about the camera and I believe they did.

The fourth study on seminars focused on eight online seminars from one class taught at Evergreen. Each class had an average of 35 students. To my knowledge, this is the first analysis of online undergraduate seminars to be published. Most research focuses on online discussions, although there are a few studies of online graduate seminars.

Besides the analyses of seminars, I present comments from a student survey, written questionnaires, workshops I gave to faculty, and faculty interviews. The survey was conducted by research assistants who asked 64 students a set of questions about seminar including whether or not they encouraged collaborative learning. The written questionnaires about seminar interaction were given to students in classes I have visited over the past 15 years. I asked students to answer this question in writing, *How do you interact in seminar?* The purpose of the questionnaires was to investigate the metaphors students used to describe their interaction. I also drew on comments and quotes from colleagues in my workshops on effective seminars that I have led over the years for my colleagues and faculty outside my college. Finally, I conducted interviews with many of the faculty whose seminars I recorded and some of their comments are included.

## BEST PRACTICES

■ Although this book is about how to teach students, it will also help you recognize your own linguistic practices and preferred facilitation style. It is not important to try all of the techniques in the best practices sections; instead, you will naturally select those that fit your own philosophy of teaching. You may find that you are more receptive to students with your own style of interacting. One of my colleagues, who is also a Buddhist priest, finds that too much talking is distracting, so he uses a small gong that he rings every fifteen minutes as a way of signaling two minutes of silence. He finds that these pauses help everyone focus more closely on the conversation. Keeping in mind that we all have different preferences for thinking and learning may help you expand your style so that you accommodate more students.

■ Teaching effective seminars has to do with designing a learning situation and modeling how to ask good questions, probing for deeper interpretations, and drawing links between ideas in the text and other readings students have done. Your own skills in modeling this work are well developed even if you have never led a seminar, because this is the work you have done to become an academic. Ask your students to pay attention to what you are doing. My former student, Amy Hitchcock, points out that for students, this is a lot to ask because they are trying to formulate their ideas, negotiate their roles, and perform their identities. Signaling what you are doing helps students focus on facilitation: *I asked that question because* or *I remember a similar idea in our reading last week.*

■ Some of the specific ways you might encourage critical thinking follow. You will find that asking just one or two of these questions is enough. In addition, there are many other sorts of questions you will need to ask, which are addressed in other chapters.

— **Clarify and elaborate.** I'm not sure I follow you. Help me understand your idea. Can someone help clarify this point?

— **Summarize.** Let's try to summarize our conversation in a couple of sentences. We can put them on the board, but first, try writing a one-sentence summary.

— **Define.** The author presents a particular definition for this word/concept/event. How do you understand it? Can you find the page where that definition occurs?

— **Hypothetical situations.** What would the consequences be if we acted on your idea? If we extended the author's argument to [describe a situation you've introduced or discussed previously in class], what might happen? Let's try a thought experiment: imagine a situation in which this idea would be true and one in which it would not.

— **Apply theory to practice.** What sorts of situations might be appropriate for this theory besides the ones mentioned in the text? What sorts of pitfalls should be taken into account given the work we've done so far in this class?

— **Critique an argument.** Where is the thesis statement in this text? What is the author's argument? What are the assumptions the author makes in making this claim? Whose perspective is highlighted? Are these assumptions valid given what we've been learning? What evidence does the author present? Can you provide more evidence for this argument from our readings so far? What is the problem the author addresses? What are the opposing views that this author presents?

— **Analogies.** What are the analogies the author uses? Is there another process that is similar to what the author is describing? Can we use the same analogy that [name author] uses for the process this author describes?

— **Compare and contrast.** How would you compare this text to the one we discussed last week? What are some of the notable differences? Besides the insights we've come up with so far, what other ideas come to mind when we look at these texts together? Let's compare this theory to [name another one].

— **Advantages and disadvantages.** What are the advantages of looking at a problem in this way? What disadvantages come to mind given our work so far?

— **Fallacies.** Part of learning critical reasoning is to examine our own conclusions. Are we avoiding the key issues this text addresses? Are we simplifying this argument/position/approach by categorizing it as ''either/or''? Are we assuming a cause and effect when actually there is only a correlation here? Have we considered all of the facts yet?

— **Persuasion.** How does the author present the information/story/argument? What are the persuasive techniques used? What are the emotional appeals and how do we react to them? What are the appeals to logic?

— **Structure or form.** How is this narrative constructed? How do the parts connect to the whole? What are the devices the author uses to create coherence?

■ Although an effective seminar would ideally include everyone's participation, the reality is that not all students participate. They may come unprepared, they may be shy, or they may not find a way to enter the conversation. Structuring the seminar so that part of the time students are working in small groups of three or four is optimal for quiet students.

■ Ask students to fill out a "Student Information Sheet" so that you will have the name they want to use in seminar, the pronoun they want to use (she, he, or a neutral pronoun such as ze), and how much experience they have in seminars. I always ask them to evaluate their ability to read for meaning and the speed of their reading as well. You may want to ask other questions as well, in order to know more about their backgrounds.

# Chapter 2

# Moving from Lectures to Seminars

Seminars open a new world to students when they discover that each text generates multiple interpretations. They also discover that there are debates in the academic community about the facts and concepts presented in them. Learning the strategies of academic inquiry is usually a new experience for students in college. It can come as a surprise to them that there are so many unanswered questions. In addition, students discover that evaluating a text is a very complex process that requires reflection about what they have learned within their own framework, as well as what other class members find important.

## LEARNING IN SEMINAR

Seminar becomes a community of practice and students learn to work together and move from peripheral participation to a central role. During that process, students need to learn what counts as a valuable contribution and how to fit it into a free-flowing conversation. Over time seminars become more collaborative and students become more proficient in understanding their collaborative nature. In (1) a student addresses these points in the following quote from a student survey:

> (1)
> I'd say I have respect for seminars now much more than I used to. I mean I definitely came here kind of still acting like I was in high school in the sense that I didn't see the benefits of seminar. I saw it more as something like a requirement that I had to find something to talk about and now I see it as something where I can, you know, hear 10 to 30 different types of opinions and viewpoints on one subject and get a much more rounded view than you can get just from a professor or yourself and I really enjoy that aspect of it.

This quote highlights the student's development as a collaborative learner, understanding that learning is about listening and not just talking. For many faculty and students who have no previous experience with seminars, the idea of talking to learn may seem strange. Inexperienced students seem to focus first on the necessity of talking without taking into consideration that the content of that talk matters more. In (2) one of my colleagues discussed his approach to a seminar on a book that all new students read during orientation week at my college:

(2)
Once I opened the forum for discussing our common text [. . .] one of the students immediately diverted our group's attention away from the text and towards a simple discussion of opinion. I was able to intervene and bring the discussion back to the text at hand, and remind people that seminar is not simply a free-for-all, but is, in fact, a self-disciplined consideration of a text, with the purpose of deep discussion and learning.

Introducing students to on-going academic conversations and encouraging them to engage in them is not just a matter of starting a conversation. This work requires a facilitator who is aware of all the dimensions of what is going on in seminar. One of these is to recognize the type of comments students offer. For example, statements of belief stop the conversation because they cannot be discussed. If a student claims that the medical establishment is a conspiracy or that green is better than blue, students are not discussing the structure of a text or its impact on a discipline, culture, or reader; instead, they are stating personal beliefs that are sometimes deeply held. By stating that seminar is a self-disciplined consideration of a text, the faculty member emphasizes that not all possible comments are relevant or useful to collaborative learning about a text.

The connection between thinking and speaking is integral to human development, and if we want students to become lifelong learners, part of their education in college needs to take that fact into account. Kenneth Bruffee (1999), in an influential book about collaborative learning, argues that we can think because we can converse. He draws from Vygotsky's theory that reflective thought is internalized conversation, and points out that we have learned to think because we are all part of communities beginning with our families, and this social nature of thought is fundamental. Conversations, then, are a central time for learning; consequently, facilitating them effectively is crucial. Bruffee writes, "If ethnocentrism, inexperience, personal anxiety, economic interest, and paradigmatic inflexibility (tunnel vision) constrain our conversation, they will constrain our thinking" (p. 134).

Understanding more about their internalized conversation is a metacognitive activity that is important for students. Part of the learning in seminar is that students reflect on their own thinking, as the following comment in (3) illustrates:

(3)

If I had an idea about what we read and how that fit into something else, to a larger thought, I could present that. This was a group of people who didn't owe me anything one way or the other, who were going to be critical of that thought. They would either say, "Oh you know, you've got holes here, here, and here," or "Hey that's good and you know maybe it could fit in to this, that, or the other." So I was able to see how my thinking was. In a lot of environments you don't get to see how you are thinking—whether or not your thinking is clear because you don't get the feedback. That was really important to me. (McCann, 2001, p. 362).

This reflection comes from a student who discovered that seminar members could teach him how to present a coherent argument. The way he explains his discovery is through reported speech, or quoting other students as they commented on his ideas. Their words support his claim and they also indicate that he listens and learns from others. He effectively demonstrates the sort of conversation I encourage in seminars, a conversation that is collegial but also critical. In (4), during a focus group discussing seminars at my college in 2012, a student focuses on everyone's work rather than her own:

(4)

I feel like things, after probably the first week in fall quarter, the material we were dealing with stopped being controversial. We just developed a sort of mutual understanding within the class that this is a communal effort [. . .] and we thus have to be very patient with each other. I think that maybe humility is what I'm trying to get at. The more communal, relational approach that we took to this inquiry allowed us to develop our own understandings as individuals, but also bounce that off our classmates constantly and be vulnerable with each other [. . .] and thus develop even more.

These two statements indicate different perspectives on learning. In (3) the male student focuses on his own development as a thinker. In (4) the female student focuses on the group's approach to seminar as communal. Both describe collaborative learning and they reveal slightly different conceptions of seminars based on gender, which I consider further in Chapter 8. They also point out important outcomes. Learning to evaluate the ways we think is how we become better thinkers. Part of being patient with each other, mentioned in (4), has to do with encountering and working with diversity in terms of hearing from students from other socioeconomic backgrounds, race, gender, abilities, sexual orientation, nationality, and age. Learning to listen to voices that are different from one's own is not easy because they can challenge the assumptions we bring to a text. They can also bring discomfort and tension. Students often mention that working across differences is hard work, but they feel that their own sociocultural awareness broadened as a result. Many begin to realize that their circles of friends and the news outlets they choose to read result in surrounding themselves with like-minded opinions. Most students begin to understand the link between learning and social interaction in a new way. The students quoted in (3) and (4) value seminar as a place for sharing tentative ideas: *this is a communal effort*. Just as important, both quotes also reveal the importance of listening.

Seminars as described in this book are free-flowing conversations that are student-centered. By student-centered, I mean that students generate the questions and determine the topics as they work collaboratively to understand a given text or problem along with the faculty members. At my college these are two-hour weekly or bi-weekly sessions involving around 25 students and one faculty member. While size may vary quite a bit, logistics are important. Participants sit in a circle or rectangle so that they can see each other, and it is best if they have a writing surface where they can also place the text under discussion. The faculty member sits with the students in the same sort of chair or desk. Arranging the room in this way illustrates the value of each person's voice.

Valuing all of the voices helps to create a community of practice where students learn to appreciate each other as thinkers and make intellectual friendships. Seminars provide an opportunity to explore their questions, learn from their peers, and gain motivation to study texts closely. It also provides a structured way to consider their prejudices, stereotypes, and values. From a cognitive perspective, students learn new ways of evaluating texts that promote analysis and synthesis. From a communications perspective, students learn to articulate their ideas in a persuasive way in order to be heard.

Feeling engaged does not come only with weekly seminars; students need to feel that their voices are valued. In a study I conducted on metaphors students used to describe seminars, many referred to the underlying metaphor IDEAS HAVE VALUE: *I put in my two bits. She contributes a lot. That was a valuable idea. What a worthless discussion. I shared my opinion.* All of these metaphorical expressions indicate that good ideas have worth, and some are worth more than others.

The students' understanding of a good seminar based on worthwhile ideas comes from practice, of course, and part of that understanding is based on informed facilitation. Effective facilitators ask for evidence from the text, they ask questions leading students to focus closely on important parts of the text, and they help students deepen the conversation, formulating new questions and new knowledge. Some people might argue that student-centered conversations take away valuable time from lectures and providing students with more information, but, in fact, learning to ask good questions is precisely the skill that all faculty members have gained in order to be part of the academy. And learning to ask good questions takes practice.

**18**

In addition, quite often the questions students raise in seminar reveal how well they understand the concepts under discussion, so they can serve as an assessment of learning. What is perhaps most startling about students' questions for the faculty member new to seminars is that almost no one expects the faculty member to answer the questions: questions are truly meant as departure points for the group to move more deeply into a text or problem or issue. In fact, many of the questions do not get answered. Open-ended inquiry can move from one question to another and that exploration is what draws us to these conversations.

## A DEVELOPMENTAL APPROACH IN HONG KONG

### Interactive Lectures

When the cultural model for school is not discussion but listening to a teacher talk, seminars may seem quite radical. This was the case when I taught in Hong Kong and gave workshops for faculty on collaborative learning. The most common question faculty members asked me was how to get students to talk when they had learned, through all of their other classroom experiences, to be passive and listen to their teachers. Most classes in Hong Kong universities follow the British model of lecture and tutorials (seminars). Because students did not talk much in tutorials, faculty members used these times in a wide variety of ways including student presentations and watching films. This situation made me reflect on how to inspire students to speak during my own class, Introduction to Sociolinguistics. I decided on a developmental approach to introduce them gradually to active participation in seminars, beginning with interactive lectures.

Part of my developmental approach included a consideration of language. I knew that the students' English was excellent because the admission to universities in Hong Kong is highly competitive. Still, English was not their first language, so I used slides containing the outline of my lectures. On the first day of class, I asked a question about an issue I had raised four minutes into my lecture. When no one volunteered to answer, I rephrased my question so that it would require a simple yes or no. When no one answered that question, I asked for a show of hands. I was amazed at how few students participated even then, and so I took a few minutes to explain that their participation in class really mattered and I was truly interested in their answers. My goal was to motivate them to engage in the class along with me. Besides articulating my expectations, I realized I would need various techniques to help all of the students feel comfortable speaking.

Although many students in Hong Kong universities characterize themselves as shy, I was fairly sure that their shyness was at least partly a product of the cultural model of what a student should be—silent. In every class after that first one, I mentioned at least one tip that would help them become better learners.

**19**

For example, I showed them how our textbook was organized and how to find what was most important. In the third week I raised the question of whether Cantonese was an endangered language given the power of Putonghua (Mandarin) as the language of the government and schools in mainland China. Several students offered opinions and two entered into a spirited conversation. I saw that asking questions that impacted their lives helped students have a good conversation even when they had gained very little theoretical background. Finding issues close to students' lives is not always possible, so I gave brief explanations about my pedagogy for all class activities to help students see that critical thinking and gaining a voice was central to our class. By the end of the 13-week semester, students were engaging in seminars. Over the course of the semester, they came to realize that there were some right answers given the research so far in linguistics, but what I wanted was something more. I wanted their critical thinking about the questions I asked based on their understanding of linguistic processes. I also wanted them to realize that there were many ways of looking at those questions, so they needed to produce a good argument based on linguistic evidence for their point of view.

Students at my college know that seminars are an integral part of the interdisciplinary classes they take so they come into our classes with curiosity about the process and some trepidation. In Hong Kong, I found that telling students that we would be having seminars in the last weeks of class produced the same effects. By designing brief interludes in my lectures when I regularly asked students to evaluate information and apply it to real situations, they could discuss the questions among themselves before hearing answers from other groups. Having regular opportunities in lectures to evaluate or apply information helped them learn the material. They were also better prepared to ask themselves questions or hypothesize about the issues. If you use this approach, my advice is that students should be allowed freedom to think. The goal is not the "right" answer; instead, it is coming up with one that seems plausible given the information they have learned so far.

Before explaining a few techniques that will inspire critical thinking during lectures, it is important to think about the reasons for lecturing. Most faculty members who lecture believe that they are conveying information directly to a student: ideas from the faculty member's brain will go directly into the students' brains. This is a common way to think about teaching: it is the transfer of knowledge. Our language reinforces this idea through common metaphors: *I didn't quite catch that idea, but I'll get it eventually. That one went right past me. The teacher didn't give me an idea of what she meant. We didn't quite grasp that concept.* These metaphors indicate our understanding of ideas—IDEAS ARE OBJECTS. Ideas can thus be caught, thrown, given, and grasped, and these actions are fast, slow, easy, or hard. If all goes well, ideas flow from brain to brain. The nature of the object (idea) can change from a ball that can be thrown (*They bounced around so many ideas I was confused*) to a sort of wall (*You hide behind your ideas*).

This notion that ideas that can be transmitted like objects is part of a larger conduit metaphor explained by the philosopher John Reddy (1979): COMMUNI-CATION IS A CONDUIT. As Reddy pointed out, the conduit metaphor is complex. We use it for understanding a text, communicating with each other, and writing. All metaphors highlight certain aspects of an object or activity, and this metaphor highlights the difficulties we have sometimes in finding the main point in a piece of writing or putting an idea into words. But the metaphor can limit the way we think about ideas and teaching and reinforce lectures as a primary teaching mode. Even if students grasp the ideas in a lecture, what do they retain? Research shows that students only retain about 10% of a lecture after three weeks if there is no review (Bligh, 2000). Instead of the conduit metaphor, we can use a builder metaphor—SEMINAR IS A BUILDING. When building, students need to find ways to build on, extend, or grapple with ideas. Asking them to do this in collaboration with others helps them realize that they can learn from each other and that more perspectives are useful.

One way to show students that SEMINAR IS A BUILDING can be a useful construct for learning is to ask them to consider what they already know about a topic before and after a lecture in order to analyze how students build on what they already know. When researchers begin with a priori notions of the content they want to see in student responses, they are often disappointed, but by beginning with the ways that students construct knowledge in their writing, they find multiple ways that students do this. In one study, researchers put students in small groups and asked students to explain online what they already understood about a topic or a question that was going to be presented by the faculty member. Researchers in psychology who have done this emphasize that students should express their beliefs or their personal experiences as ways of activating their prior knowledge (Lester & Paulus, 2011). The students post again after the lecture, contrasting what they have learned in the lecture to this prior knowledge. By working in groups and responding to each other's blogs, students can see their own thinking transformed. The lecturer can also skim these to see what students have learned. I discuss metaphors and how they can inform our practice more extensively in Chapter 5.

In the first weeks of my class in Hong Kong, I interspersed five types of activities into my lectures:

- "Think-pair-share." This is probably the most well-known activity for large lectures. The faculty member poses a question for students to consider in a brief period of time, say one minute. Next, they turn to the student next to them to discuss their ideas for another minute. Finally, a few students self-select to report out. The advantage of this sort of pause in the lecture is for students to verify their understanding of the material, and the lecturer can modify the lecture to match this understanding.

- An activity I have named "Ask-don't-tell" can be used as a sort of priming activity. Instead of stating reasons for a phenomenon, steps in a process, or problems with a theory, ask the students to do this in small groups (three to four students) first. This is called priming because it has a sort of memory effect. You are asking students to consider what might come next in your lecture, and then after they report out from brief small group discussions, they will see their own hypotheses confirmed, elaborated upon, or rejected. In short, they will care about what comes next in the lecture. They may remember it better as well.

- Brainstorming is another activity that is actually a generative device. It is useful for finding creative ways to solve a problem, list solutions, next steps, or generate research questions. In this exercise students in pairs or small groups work together to list as many possibilities, solutions, or next steps as possible, and to do so very quickly. One student volunteers to record the results as well as participate in the brainstorm. The recorder writes down all responses and no one is allowed to evaluate or question any of them. It is only a listing activity. After doing this for one to two minutes, the group can select one or two of the responses and develop them further either in the small group or in the larger class.

- Problem-solving tasks. These can be useful when students already have background information about a particular issue. You can ask students to work in groups of two to three and divide the class into five sections. Each section considers a single aspect of the problem, namely what resources, data, skills, environments, or stakeholders may be necessary to solve the issue. This is a useful exercise as preparation for reading a case study and helping students apply theory to real world problems.

- The one minute note card. Students get a note card where they write one important thing they have learned and, if they wish, one question. By reviewing these note cards, which takes very little time, I tailored my next lecture to review concepts that were difficult. When I did this, students were thrilled to have their questions answered, and they signaled to those around them that they had provided the question. I used them in part to assess class participation because the comments indicate what they found "important." If it is a minor point or something you mentioned only in passing, that could be an indication of poor preparation or poor listening skills. Students learn to write succinct statements that link ideas they are reading and hearing in lecture. This practice helps them prepare for seminar as well.

Most lecturers include some discussion, and this can be for student's questions or the faculty member can provide a number of questions. But what happens in discussions? Researchers have found that faculty members talk more than students, and they tend to filter the talk so that they direct and orchestrate the conversation. They take more frequent turns and these turns are longer than students' turns (Kramarae & Treichler, 1990). By directing the discussion, lecturers maintain control over the content. This is useful in some ways because the lecturer can reiterate points or provide alternative explanations for a point already presented. It is possible not to fully appreciate a student's question, however, unless it is well formed or based on the lecture in some clearly defined way. In addition, students may feel less inclined to speak in a public forum where each person's question or answer is immediately evaluated by the faculty member. Students who are shy, unfamiliar with academic discourse, or are nonnative speakers of English may not feel they can express themselves clearly. These factors can reduce the number of students who participate and the topics that are addressed.

## Workshops

Transforming discussion periods into a time for student-centered learning where students are interacting with each other rather than with the lecturer, can be done through workshops. Workshops, in the sense I am using the term here, are structured experiences created by the faculty member and designed to test students' understanding of a text or concept in a collaborative way. The faculty member provides questions, listing a period of time for the students to respond, and then the students take over. They form groups of five to eight, and designate a recorder so that at the end of the workshop, at least one person in each group is prepared to summarize the group's discussion on each question for the whole class. I taught students how to conduct field work in sociolinguistics using this method. First, I gave them an assignment to survey people about their attitudes about Cantonese, Mandarin, and English. I included a list of questions for the survey and explained research questions. Instead of lecturing about all the issues students would need to consider as they administered the survey, I handed out questions and students worked together in small groups to come up with the best procedures.

Here are the questions I asked:

1. Who should you ask to take part in your study and why?
2. Why should you tell your participants that their answers will be confidential? Give at least three reasons.
3. Why should you ask the same questions in the same order and in the same way?

4. What might be the best method for writing down the responses? Explain why your method is the best.
5. What sort of location would be best for the informant when you ask these questions? Think about public and private spaces.
6. Why is it important to tell your participants that you will not keep their responses to the questions after we complete our survey?

Students had a time limit of 20 minutes, so they realized that they needed detailed, thoughtful responses. Each group worked on the same questions. At the end of the 20 minutes, I called on one group to answer each question. Students who wanted to add information in that final discussion period were free to do so. Even though students were familiar with several field research methodologies, they had not yet conducted a survey. Considering the factors that contribute to a good protocol in the workshop helped them see that, as researchers, they needed to adhere to that protocol in order to gather valid data. Because they were involved at the beginning of the project, they raised important questions throughout the process. The students were very good at tallying their results, but what was more exciting to me were their reflections about how to improve the project. They were learning to evaluate methodology and seeing its relevance to researching questions.

Workshops are also useful for understanding difficult concepts and they require careful consideration of learning goals. "Conceptual workshops" ask students to define concepts, apply them to various situations in the text or in their lives, and then compare these different situations in order to refine their understanding of the concept. To explain this approach further, I will draw on Finkel (2000, pp. 98–100) because he introduced this type of workshop to our college. He provides an explanation of a conceptual workshop on Socrates' way of responding to "aporia," a philosophical puzzle or impasse. The workshop begins by asking students to define aporia through an inductive process. To do this Finkel first provides six passages from Plato's dialogues where aporia appears, and asks students to describe what the similarities are in each passage. The goal in this first step is to define aporia by seeing how it is described in different ways. The second step is to ask students to find out what Socrates does in each of the six moments he has listed. In one case, for example, Socrates just goes on with the argument. In the third step, Finkel asks students to compare and contrast Socrates' way of responding to aporia. The workshop ends with another quote from the *Symposium* that students analyze in light of this work. Finkel explains that his goals were for students to identify aporia in the texts and demonstrate how these moments functioned dramatically and psychologically.

Another type of workshop I have developed is not based on a task or major concept; instead, it is designed to unpack a number of complex ideas in a textbook. For years I have used Eckert and McConnell-Ginet's (2003) *Language and gender* in undergraduate classes at all levels, although it is best suited to upper division work. Unlike many textbooks, there are no discussion questions. I created workshops on each chapter with questions that asked students to define and compare concepts, and to find examples from their own experiences. I place students in small groups for about 50 minutes to answer four questions. I circulate among the groups to hear their progress and note who is contributing. Then, in the whole group we listen to each group's findings, summarizing as we go through the questions. These weekly workshops set up expectations that students will need to define concepts in their own words and test them with theory and their own experiences. They become astute observers and listeners in their daily lives; in short, they become budding linguists.

Workshops promote a noisy atmosphere of inquiry and collaboration, where students have the opportunity to work together to understand complex questions their faculty members have written. They are tightly organized by the faculty member, and particularly well suited to testing hypotheses and guided inquiry. To create them, you transform lectures into questions based on the texts in your class. Students understand that they are directly engaging the concepts and they are challenged and sometimes stumped. In all my years of teaching, however, I have found that they persist until they have come up with a response. They know other students are working on the same questions and they can see the work proceeding around the room, which provides motivation.

After completing two or more of these workshops, many students understand that each of them have perspectives to offer and that these can be valuable. They learn to trust their peers to have information or insights and they learn to build on each other's ideas. They also begin to know each other as thinkers because small groups permit each student to contribute. These points are critical in seminars where the faculty member is primarily a facilitator.

## Seminars

Like workshops, seminars may not be orderly and rational and student's comments may not always be well phrased using academic discourse. With many possible voices, you will hear overlapping voices, half-formed ideas, quickly changing topics, tangents, and some confusion. On the other hand, you will also hear perceptive comments, sudden inspiration, excitement, and novel ideas. Some students will feel very comfortable speaking and some may be silent; some will express controversial or offensive opinions; some may be afraid to raise an opposing point of view. These are issues I focus on in later chapters, and they are not easy to resolve or even recognize. What I focus on is helping students gain a voice.

By voice I mean two things: the literal definition of saying something out loud and the metaphorical one of offering a particular perspective as a result of personal experience, intellectual preparation, and critical thinking in the context of what others are saying. Voice has to do with the content of a comment, the way the comment fits into the conversation, and the way the comment is shaped. Part of developing a voice, then, is learning strategic and persuasive ways of offering ideas. It is not enough to have the ideas in the first place. Because seminar is an improvisation, timing a comment is essential. Because students are getting to know each other, they are negotiating their identities with each other. And, because they are learning collaboratively, they are negotiating power and solidarity.

Part of this negotiation has to do with making sure everyone's voice is included to avoid the sense of marginalization some students have in seminars. This is a primary job for the facilitator. Being marginalized is not part of the peripheral participation in a community of practice; instead, it is a feeling of being silenced and having no power to affect the conversation. Researchers examining silencing find that students' perception of how their ideas will be received has long-term effects on their participation in class and in their lives. In one study, students' reports of their own political identification in relation to their instructors' were examined for effects on classroom climate. When students perceived that their instructor had dissimilar political attitudes and opinions, they did not feel that the classroom climate was unsupportive of their views unless the instructors were perceived to engage in silencing behaviors. There were no significant differences between students who were left or right on the political spectrum (Henson & Denker, 2007). Although silencing behaviors were not listed, these could include cutting students off, joking about particular views, assuming a common point of view, and making disparaging comments. In my experience, some students perceive they are being silenced even though they have contributed major points because they want to convince others.

In workshops, questions are written by the faculty. In seminars, students generate the questions. Upon hearing this, faculty members ask how they can inspire their students to have in-depth, exciting conversations about the texts. The first step in creating effective seminars is to help students see that the conversation is not about winning a debate or an argument, nor is it mere speculation; instead, seminar is a collaborative search for understanding a text within the context of your class. For a seminar to be an effective learning experience, everyone needs to participate in some way. Merely inviting students to have a conversation without some sort of structure, though, can be disastrous. In Hong Kong I began by dividing my class into small groups and providing them with the same five questions. These were open-ended questions and I emphasized that there were many possible perspectives. I set a time limit so that we could review each of the questions together. Not surprisingly, in those groups students raised other questions, and sometimes those became more central to their conversations than the ones I had posed. I encouraged this practice.

26

## PREPARING TO TEACH SEMINARS

In a study I conducted on my campus, I found five basic elements necessary to teaching effective seminars: (1) choosing appropriate texts, (2) deciding on an explicit goal, (3) helping students prepare, (4) developing seminar rules, and (5) using an appropriate assessment method (Fiksdal, 2001). The best seminar texts have depth and enduring importance because of the topics or themes they address. Textbooks are self-contained with their own objectives and explanations, so unless you are studying them from a particular perspective, they may be less useful. If you assign an advanced or complex text, students need to be well prepared to address it. If they are not well prepared, assigning key parts, or creating a workshop to cover some of the essential concepts might be more appropriate. In interdisciplinary classes when students are using a number of genres to understand a problem or question, having a seminar on a single history text, for example, can pose difficulties for students because students tend to believe that the text tells them everything they need to know. Unless they are exposed to the complexity of the historical events in terms of the social, economic, and cultural background of the time, they may find it difficult to discern a point of view. Films can also be difficult to use as a text if students have no background on how to "read" a film.

The text you choose should be complex, multi-layered, perhaps controversial, and open to interpretation. If the text is too long, many students will not complete the reading. I usually assign no more than 200 pages for a seminar. If the text is longer, you can ask students to focus on particular sections or have more than one seminar on the book. Another approach is to select multiple texts (or parts of one text) and announce a "jigsaw" seminar. In this type of seminar, students assemble an understanding of the text(s) from the parts. You divide students into reading groups, each of which will read a different text. Seminar begins with differnt groups composed of at least two students from each of the reading groups. Their job is to explain what they learned from their text and to learn from each of the other students about their text. Then, in larger groups of 10–15 students they can generate questions and begin to discuss themes, concepts, and ideas they generated in the small groups. Finally, students can report on their most important findings to the whole group.

Announcing a goal for seminar helps guide the conversation. This can be a very broad goal, such as understanding the author's argument and how it relates to other readings in your class. Another goal can be to study a topic collectively by specializing. Specializing in this case means that students choose an area or topic in which they will become an expert. A colleague in literature at my college asked each student what was most important to them in reading a piece of literature. If they chose characterization, he asked them to prepare for seminar focusing on that aspect. Each student had a focus for seminar and each gained an expertise in

**27**

the area that interested them most over the academic term. Some colleagues have used this idea in scientific seminars as well. If students are studying water quality, they may specialize in various aspects such as research methodologies, public health, or microorganisms and when they discuss research articles or a book, they present their ideas using their expertise. Seminars can be venues for creative work as well, so if the goal is to understand a play or dialogue, students could role play for a period of time and then reflect on that experience.

Helping students prepare for seminars is a key part of teaching effectively. Many students find it hard to finish the reading and even if they have, they feel unprepared for an in-depth conversation. Faculty members can provide students with some guiding questions as they read, and these can be the first questions to discuss in seminar. Possibly the best preparation I have found is to give a writing assignment. Writing a one paragraph summary and a one paragraph response about a topic that is important in the text can help students reflect on what they have read. I assign these two-paragraph essays and require students to post them on our class webpage by midnight the day before seminar. This allows most students time to read a variety of responses before they come to seminar. Some students complain that they changed their ideas in seminar, and they don't want the pre-seminar assignment to be their last word on the text. I make sure to give other, integrative assignments in which they can provide a more sophisticated point of view about the text after seminar, which helps them demonstrate their learning. The point of writing prior to seminar is to help students reflect on what they've read and articulate ideas. Writing prior to seminar prepares students to link their ideas to the text in seminar, and it helps them respond more readily to other students.

The next part of the preparation is to create the rules for seminar or a seminar covenant. In our first seminar, I like to ask students to generate rules as a group while I write them on the board. I try to use the words students offer and prompt them to make a list of eight to ten rules to guide our collaborative work. I put the rules on the class webpage, and hand them out in class. It is useful to ask students to look over the rules from time to time. In a recent team-taught course, one of my colleagues suggested that we ask our students to choose one of the rules and practice it. At the end of class, we asked students to comment about which rule they followed. This provided students an indirect way of paying attention to the rules they created and to deepen the social contract they created by making the rules. Some students reported that because we wanted to hear from everyone, they spoke up rather than remain silent. More talkative students were also careful to monitor their comments because of the same rule.

## ASSESSING STUDENTS IN SEMINAR

Assessing students can be difficult because if you are facilitating and joining the conversation, it is easy to focus on content alone. I emphasize that each student has a responsibility towards collaborative learning. I make a practice of taking notes about the topics with the student's name and the nature of their comments. That means that most of the time I am writing. Students looking to me to answer a question or provide commentary soon give up because I'm busy. They learn to rely on the group. I do not subscribe to the idea that talking a lot should be highly valued; instead, I emphasize to the students that seminar is about careful listening. I focus on whether or not students are making substantive contributions to seminar, and how they are doing that. Some, for example, are good at probing ideas and helping to deepen the conversation, some are good at asking questions, some are good at applying concepts to real world problems. Some help draw others into the conversation. Some are excellent summarizers. Ideally, students learn all these skills. They can assess their own seminar work if you provide them with a rubric.

## CONCLUSION

It is important to remember that in seminar students are preoccupied with sorting out their own analysis of a question or problem, understanding other students' perspectives, and creating a coherent understanding of all of these ideas. Faculty members are often most concerned with the quality of the ideas and when faced with unfocused notions, hazy intuitions, and cloudy connections, they may despair. By focusing on what is going on rather than what we wish would go on, it is easier to assess students' work. That is, be aware of the students as learning the practice of academic discourse over time with each text presenting new difficulties. Besides this struggle with content, students are also aware of the group and they are presenting various identities and using power and solidarity to achieve their own goals as a member of an on-going community of practice.

## BEST PRACTICES

■ In your first seminar, take the time to let students introduce themselves to the group. Explain that together you are creating a learning community so it is important to know each other. I encourage students to learn each other's names, and I learn everyone's name as well. Create seminar rules so that everyone knows the ground rules. I ask the students for suggestions, and I add one or two if necessary. I then type them up and post them on our website. Here are the rules from one of my recent seminars:

— Come prepared.

— Respect other people's opinions.

— Have tolerance for others—it's a learning community.

- — Speak in a way that is not demeaning.
- — Try not to interrupt.
- — Stay on task.
- — Try not to monopolize the conversation.
- — Encourage quiet people to voice their thoughts.
- — Be open-minded.
- — Questioning or disagreeing is okay.
- — Show that you are listening by referring to comments made by others.

■ Some students are unfamiliar with academic conversations. You can hand out this list of ways to participate (Marshall & Roland, 2013). Emphasize to your students that with practice, they will develop more approaches, particularly if they are good listeners.

- — Listen closely most of the time. Contribute one idea that you have reflected on, or a piece of information.
- — Attempt to paraphrase what another student has said to make sure you understood them.
- — Ask questions that begin with *Do you mean that; What do you think about; Why?*
- — Express support for another student's idea and explain why you find it useful.

■ Providing a structure for each seminar will help develop a sense of community and trust in the work of inquiry. I always divide students into groups for at least 15 minutes, making sure they work in groups of different sizes each week. Assigning students randomly is my choice, but it can be useful to divide students into talkers and non-talkers or those who have finished the text and those who have not. Usually, I only have to divide them once in groups of those who have prepared and those who have not, because students in the unprepared group see that they are in a very small minority. Recently, I did this and worked mostly with the students who had not read the text. We worked on some passages by doing close reading, and they found this very productive because the text was too difficult for them. The groups need a clear assignment or focus and time limit.

■ If students have not prepared questions prior to class, you can ask them to work in groups of three to write open-ended questions (not those that can be answered with yes or no) for discussion in the first 10 minutes of class. One person in each group writes their question on the board whenever their group is ready. I nominate a student sitting close to the board to read all of the questions. Then, I ask students to choose one to start our conversation, and I wait for a first comment.

- When I divide students into groups, I visit the groups to listen to the conversation for three to four minutes each, taking notes about the topic and who is talking. My colleague, Toska Olson, notes that if students do not seem to be working well together, it is important to ask how they are doing. If you do not hear a clear response, it is a good idea to speak with the students individually after class. Some may not have read the text, or a student may be disrupting the work. Typically, students will be forthcoming if you speak with them individually.

- In my studies of seminars, students emphasize that the faculty member should play a clear role. Some reported faculty members saying, "This is your seminar, so I won't talk." This is a very poor technique because the students want to hear from the faculty member. Students also criticize faculty who give mini lectures during seminar. This practice implies that the students are not capable of working with the text. Giving your students time to work through their ideas and questions sets the stage for deeper learning. Teaching a seminar means being a member of the group and offering comments or asking questions from time to time. Try to limit your substantive questions to three at most. Your participation should model an effective, academic approach to the conversation.

- Most important to effective teaching in seminars is exploring the text in some depth. It can be hard to find a balance between tangents and ideas directly focused on the text, but allowing some exploration is worthwhile so that the group can make new connections and find new perspectives. For this reason it is very important not to comment after each student's comment. Allow students to work on ideas together and enter the conversation to help them dig deeper. One way to do this is by asking the group to make an idea more precise and to connect it to other class materials: *How can we state this idea in one sentence using the terminology we've been learning? This idea seems related to last week's lecture on X and Y. What do you think?*

- Students can be facilitators after they have some experience with seminars. Some of my colleagues create teams of two to three students who plan the structure. In a smaller class, individual students can facilitate. This practice does not mean that the faculty member can or should remain silent. There are times when student facilitators may not have the power or authority or expertise to move students out of a dead end, an argument, or a tangent. When I need to do this, I always use *us* rather than *you*. For example, I might say, *we seem to have wandered far afield. Let's move to our next question so that we continue exploring the ideas in the text.* This use of *we* indicates that faculty member and students alike are responsible for seminar.

- One way to help students prepare for seminar is to show them how you do it. I have shown students how I mark the text and how I take notes for seminar. You can ask them what practices they use as well.

**31**

■ In our final 10 minutes of the conversation, I often use a round robin in which each seminar member briefly states a conclusion or a point they wanted to make earlier. The round robin allows each student to speak in turn around the circle and they can pass if they wish. I encourage passing if a student has already contributed a lot. I encourage quiet or silent students to contribute rather than pass. If seminar is new to students, using the round robin to ask students to comment on process can be useful.

■ At the end of seminar it may be useful to provide a brief summary of the topics and ask students to write for three minutes about what they learned. If you do this regularly, students will be thinking about their learning during seminar—a good focus.

■ Using a rubric to assess students in seminar can be useful. As shown in Table 2.1, a rubric outlines each element of your assessment and provides a quick way to chart their progress. I learned to create rubrics only recently when I team-taught with Sunshine Campbell, a colleague in education. For her, every move we made in our class needed to be intentional and planned. After a couple of weeks of relentless questions about our assignments, I finally grasped the point. Intentionality is important because if students question your methodology or try to revolt, you can explain very clearly why you are asking them to do something. Rubrics force you to think about learning outcomes and articulate the ways you will conduct assessment. Giving the rubric to your students at the beginning of your class helps them understand the conversational moves that are valued in collaborative learning. I suggest assessing each student twice during the term. Use one copy of the rubric and write the student's name in the comments box for each element you notice. This can be done using just one copy of the rubric each time if you don't have too many students. You can also ask students to evaluate themselves by handing out the rubric and using the last five minutes of your time period. In this case, they should provide paraphrases of the statements or questions or observations that they made so that you have the evidence for their achievement. By using a rubric, you focus your students' attention on learning and you clarify the process.

*Table 2.1* Rubric for Seminar Assessment

| Level of Proficiency | Category of Idea | Comments/Evidence |
|---|---|---|
| Proficient | — Brings theory from text or other class materials to bear on ideas<br>— Contributes a new idea or asks a fruitful question based on good analysis<br>— Comments indicate some original synthesis of ideas<br>— Listens carefully and summarizes ideas or makes connections between them<br>— Disagrees showing respect for other students' points of view<br>— Expresses ideas clearly and succinctly<br>— Consistently shows responsibility for learning | |
| Meeting Minimal Requirements | — Provides some analysis of the text<br>— Tests understanding of a theory in the text by explaining it<br>— Provides evidence from the text for ideas presented<br>— Listens to other students and builds on their ideas<br>— Asks for clarification or explanations of major points<br>— Most ideas and comments are well explained | |
| Beginning | — Agrees or disagrees minimally with the author or another student<br>— Asks a question which indicates superficial reading of the text<br>— Participation varies widely from seminar to seminar<br>— Contributions are not always clearly stated<br>— Silent but some learning is apparent in other forums | |

## Chapter 3

# Power and Ways of Talking

Conversations are the way we begin learning about the world. From our first moments as babies, we interact with our parents and caregivers and our gestures, sounds, and facial expressions are considered to be meaningful. This focus on conversation, and attention to both sounds and gestures, reveals the importance we place on conversation for understanding each other. From birth through to adulthood, we quickly learn how to engage in all sorts of conversations with family, friends, teachers, and bosses and these conversations have lots of purposes. We cement friendships, solve problems, have arguments, and, importantly, we can all recall conversations that have taught us something. In fact, education itself can be considered a conversational process, both with others and internally, with ourselves.

In college, many researchers point to the importance of "entering the conversation" as a way of learning. Seminars in a college setting draw on this way of thinking about conversation: it is a time to engage with others about important ideas in the context of class materials. Importantly, seminars are created only by our language. In a way, we establish seminars by putting "seminar" on our syllabus, and arranging the room so that we can see each other, but it is the nature of our conversation that creates a seminar. One of my colleagues asked his students to talk as though they were in seminar to test that notion, and everyone recognized typical phrases. The purpose of seminar is collaborative learning. As one of my students put it, "I wouldn't even say you're learning to work *in* a group, you're learning to work *as* a group." As we facilitate, we need to be aware of multiple ways of talking so that dominant voices are not the only contributors. These dominant voices can become very powerful over time stopping others from getting the floor, or silencing ideas that they do not sanction.

The complexity of the conversations in seminar may not be immediately obvious because we converse all of the time. Students may think that all they need to do is talk to impress the faculty—lots of talk will result in a favorable assessment. Faculty members may assume that all students need to do is talk about the academic content of the course and critical thinking will begin to happen. Neither of these perspectives will create an effective seminar. Listening is just as important as voicing an opinion, and students need guidance in order to move toward critical thinking. Another common perception is that the conversation is good if relevant ideas are raised, and the threads of conversation are being developed in some detail. Focusing only on well-formed ideas and incisive analysis means that you may be overlooking other learning that is occurring. The questions, momentary confusion, tangents, and dead ends are all part of learning because they are evidence of active engagement in the ideas. Testing the ideas, trying to link them to other class materials, and doing that collaboratively is part of a very powerful process.

This process of collaborative learning is messy. It can include breathtaking generalizations or details of one student's personal experience that are only tenuously related to the topic at hand. And, it can include very articulate, well-reasoned contributions. Once seminar participants hear this range of comments, they begin to realize that they need to examine what they really think, not just what they have assumed to be true. They begin to realize that putting forth one's own analysis is worth far more than merely repeating what they have heard from others. Who has not felt the thrill of putting an idea into words and having others treat those ideas as useful or even insightful?

## TAKING RISKS TO GAIN A VOICE

This process of testing ideas is risky and we can all remember moments of trepidation when we spoke out or decided to remain silent in class. Over the years, I have tried to help students learn that they should not abandon an idea merely because no one commented on it. Everyone is preoccupied. Some participants are trying to follow the conversation, some find that a previous comment triggered an idea and they are trying to retrieve that idea, some are thinking about what they want to say, some are thinking about lunch. Voicing ideas does not mean merely formulating an idea into words. It is important to take the time to relate the idea to the conversation and say enough about the idea so that others have time to orient to it.

In this respect, the ways we talk are just as integral to the experience as the ideas expressed. Does the speaker explain the idea in enough detail that everyone can understand? Who is talking? Is it someone who often speaks or someone who usually does not? Are the primary speakers encouraging others to engage in the conversation? Seminars open the way for students to take responsibility for their own learning—to engage with a text or experience it on their own terms, to gain a voice. At the same time, that conversation occurs in a social, economic, psychological, and political context where social identities are constructed moment by moment. These are not always neutral activities. On my campus, for example, students of color report that they hear racist comments and that these comments do not always seem to be noticed by others. Of course it is not only students of color who may feel embattled. Those who hold unpopular or unexamined views, those who cling too long to a position that no one else supports, those who have to fight to get a word in edgewise—any student may at times feel that seminar has become a struggle. This is especially true if others have not noticed the struggle.

It may seem that if there are seminar rules for civil conversation, everyone will be protected, but this notion is ideologically based. That is, the way we think about civility in conversation has to do with what we believe is commonly understood. If the majority of the students in your seminars are white and heterosexual they may not notice that their comments are racist or otherwise offensive. The dominant group of any race or ethnicity may feel that anyone having an objection will speak up, but this is not a simple matter. Comments can be understood in very different ways, depending on each person's perceptions. Should a Native American faculty member intervene in the conversation when students speak of the United States as an "immigrant nation"? Doesn't this phrase ignore the indigenous peoples already living here when immigrants arrived? Doesn't it ignore the multitudes of slaves that did not ask to come? Doesn't it ignore the Mexicans who suddenly found themselves in another country after the Mexican-American War?

If the faculty member chooses not to say anything, will students of the same heritage or other backgrounds wonder about that choice? What about the students who are part of the dominant majority in this country? Wouldn't they learn more if the faculty member intervened? And, why should this role fall on the faculty member? Shouldn't students raise this important point themselves? Choosing to speak up has to do with constructing and highlighting identity, so the choice is not inconsequential. Students who are queer or shy or who have an accent can feel shut down by a particular comment. And, once a seminar participant does speak up, the reaction among others is just as important. If other group members do not seem to accept this point as relevant, the faculty member or student can feel that their power and voice in seminar has been minimized.

## POWER IN CONVERSATIONS

Power in conversations has to do with agency, or the ability to make a conversational move. It is part of any seminar as it is in any conversation because agency is necessary for anything to happen at all (Johnstone, 2002). That means students have the power to give voice to an idea or question. There is a measure of power in that move. Other moves we are more likely to associate with power are controlling the floor or talking a lot. Students can also gain power by making controversial statements, using debate techniques, arguing to win, or using derisive tones that silence others. These moves can create asymmetrical relationships. Students can gain power by making articulate, thoughtful contributions as well. Power is fluid in seminar if everyone keeps in mind the motivating goal of collaborative learning. If learning is central, then working on hearing from everyone is vital. Recognizing this common goal is a counterbalance to the power of an individual because it is a mutual orientation to shared knowledge and it highlights solidarity in the group.

An important part of learning in seminar has to do with recognizing others' voices and hearing their reactions to what is being said. And, it can be difficult to appreciate the full import of what a student is saying. If you do not have the same background or experiences as the speaker, the weight of some ideas may seem light. Allowing students to develop a voice is important and that development begins with their actually voicing an opinion or asking a question. Even a short statement can give students a sense that speaking is part of the collaboration. With experience, students can present an analysis, link their ideas to other students' ideas, and present a synthesis based on their own interpretations. Most important to students is that they are largely responsible for the content and direction of the conversation. It can be both exciting and daunting to enter into a seminar because of this unusual responsibility. Generally speaking, most of the schooling in kindergarten through middle school is very highly controlled by the authority of teachers. In the college seminar, however, the conversation is much freer because the idea of inquiry is foremost.

This de-centering of authority gives students time to grapple with the reading. They experience integrative learning when they encounter ideas that challenge their thinking and can explore ideas they may not have considered previously. These ideas do not develop in a linear fashion because they are formulated, reformulated, questioned, tinkered with, pulled apart, and placed in new juxtapositions with other ideas as a result of the group's collective work.

## THE NATURE OF COLLABORATIVE LEARNING

It is not always possible to know if seminars provide new learning with so much going on. In one of my studies, I asked students if they thought their seminar was successful. I followed that with a probe: *How do you know if collaborative learning is taking place?* Many students said that they had new ideas as a result of the conversation. In (1) a student describes the process:

(1)
This kind of pushing deeper into the issue beyond just the surface level happens when people are entertaining each other's perspectives. And when you're entertaining someone else's perspective and you're taking it in [. . .] and [. . .] pushing it around in your mind, I think you are learning from that

person. You're learning from that perspective [. . .] and by virtue of it being a collaborative process it's collaborative learning.

In (2) another pointed out the learning she experienced may not occur when struggling with an idea alone:

(2)
My problem is that it's hard for me to articulate things. Someone else will say something I was sort of vaguely thinking about and they'll put it in actual words. So when someone—when that happens for me then I feel that I'm getting something out of the process personally.

Sometimes seminars provide moments of a collective "ah hah" that is exciting to everyone. I captured one of these moments on videotape. Students were discussing Michael Dorris' *A Yellow Raft in Blue Water*. In (3) I present comments from different students about that moment:

(3)
- I'm just amazed that we come up with these ideas. I mean I'm just like sitting here and listening and thinking wow, you know, I never in a million years would have thought of half of this stuff.

- I think that Sky sums it up best on page 97: 'Hey man everything means something. There ain't nothin' that's an accident.'

In each of these comments we find aspects of collaborative learning: students working together can come up with ideas that an individual working alone could not; and looking for patterns in a novel reveals the craft of writing that might escape a reader who is merely following a plot line. But these comments reveal much more if we look closely at how students phrase their comments. The students are also pointing to identity, face, and solidarity in a collective improvisation. In the first comment, the student says, "I'm just amazed that we come up with these ideas." The "we" clearly indicates that it is the group as a whole that is contributing to the ideas, not certain individuals. The student then says, "I mean I'm just like sitting here." Her use of "like" signals her social identity as young and cool. She then quotes herself: "[. . .] thinking wow, you know, I never in a million years would have thought of half of this stuff." This is an example of reported speech—we report on what we or someone else said or thought by quoting, and it gives her a measure of authority. Her use of "you know" marks solidarity with the group: you know what I know. This solidarity move also gives face to the group. By giving face I mean that she reinforces the positive value of collaborating together: everyone gains face or reputation in the group by participating in an effective seminar.

In the second comment, the student quotes one of the characters and gives the page number. By doing this he is giving his idea more weight because he refers to the authority of the text and not only to what he thinks. This indicates that he knows the text well and can connect a character's statement with the group's achievement and this type of connection points to the authority of a knowledgeable student. Connecting ideas has high value in seminar. This brief analysis of the discourse reveals what is going on with just two comments and previews topics in the remaining chapters.

Not all seminars have "ah hah" moments, so how do we know students are learning? In one of my studies, undergraduate research assistants surveyed randomly selected students. Of the 64 students they queried, all but three said they thought collaborative learning did occur in their seminars. Responses were diverse, but can be collectively paraphrased as follows:

> Everyone is receptive to new ideas or perspectives, and there is a certain harmony and comfort in the group. During the discussion, most people contribute different ideas or perspectives. These ideas are discussed in depth and there is a sense that the group is synthesizing or piecing a puzzle together. People can talk about what they learned outside of class and they believe they have encountered new ideas or changed their opinions somewhat.

There are, of course, moments of confusion, or entire sections of seminars that don't seem to be productive. One reason these seminars may seem unproductive is that the conversation is not always coherent, rational, and articulate. But there is another reason some faculty may not see learning, and that is vague or incoherently expressed ideas. What is valued is articulateness. As a student of literature, language, and linguistics, I have always valued articulateness. I believe this value was reinforced when I studied in France for two years. College-educated people there expect articulate speech of public speakers and even their friends. One of my French friends, for example, admired former president François Mitterrand because he used the imperfect subjunctive on occasion. This notion is worth exploring. What do academics mean by articulate speech?

## GOOD AND BAD ENGLISH

First, articulate speech usually means using Standard English; second, it refers to well-expressed and thoughtful ideas; and finally, it can refer to careful pronunciation. Standard English is based on prescriptive rules found in grammar books but it is not spoken. It is an idealized, unchanging English with no accent. This version of English can be found in academic writing but not all published pieces. If you consider the complaints of language mavens about the state of English today, this becomes obvious because they point out grammar rules that writers and speakers are not following. Yet, three of the most important characteristics of spoken language are that it changes from place to place, speaker to speaker and over time. Everywhere that English is spoken, there are many varieties or dialects. In the United States, we recognize southern or Texan as well as British, Australian, and Indian English. We also adapt the ways we speak depending on the circumstances. In the south, *you all* is an accepted way of indicating that *you* is plural. I am not from the south, but I find it easy to adopt this practice when I visit. Rules and practices also shift over time. Even though *ain't* was widely used, it was declared nonstandard by nineteenth-century grammarians, and today we have the sense that it is not correct English. If we go back further in time and read *The Canterbury tales* by Chaucer, we realize that English in the fourteenth century was vastly different.

Some readers might be thinking, "Hold on, I speak Standard English!" If you record and transcribe every word you speak, though, you will see that it is hard to use Standard English in every conversation. What about talking to a child or your best friend? Is *have a good one* Standard English? It turns out that Standard English is not the English anyone routinely uses, even in seminar. We don't always speak in complete sentences, as the transcriptions in this book will illustrate. We combine words such as *going to* as *gonna*, we say *yeah* rather than *yes*, we use slang and pop-culture expressions such as *that's a no-brainer*, we may use profanity, and we all have accents and speak a dialect. The term "mainstream English" is a more accurate term for the English used in colleges, courts, government, and business.

It is important to consider the consequences of teaching students to aspire to an idealized way of speaking and writing, which is a major activity in most educational institutions. This belief that ideas worth hearing must be phrased in Standard English is a language ideology or an assumption we hold that seems to be common sense. We may not always be aware of language ideologies, but they underlie our everyday behavior and our conversational practices. I have talked to students who felt less intelligent than others because they did not speak mainstream English, and this feeling was consistently reinforced throughout their schooling. Once they understand that the way they speak is a variety or dialect, and that it has grammatical rules just as Standard English does, they realize their language is just as good as anyone else's. It may have less prestige in seminar, but it has high prestige among their friends and in other communities of practice. It is quite possible, of course, to learn mainstream English.

Before discussing the relationship of language and power further, I will explain what linguists mean by "dialect" and "accent." Dialects are varieties of a language. They are different ways of speaking one language and they differ from each other because of vocabulary, grammar, and pronunciation. Generally, they are intelligible to speakers of a particular language, but there can be times when they are not. In the United States there are many dialects. New York, Boston, and a few other large cities have several; there are southern dialects, and Appalachian, to list a few examples of geographical dialects. Dialects can also be used by social groups across geographical areas. There are rural dialects and working class dialects. In one early and well known study, a linguist asked clerks where an article of clothing was located in three different New York department stores, each catering to three different social classes. The article had to be on the fourth floor, so the sociolinguist could determine who pronounced the r in the words "fourth floor." He found that clerks in the high-end store pronounced r in both words while those in the inexpensive store tended to drop r in both words. It is more prestigious to pronounce r in New York City, so that is why clerks in the high-end store spoke more like their upper middle class customers (Labov, 1972). This is an example of social stratification in language and it indicates that we signal our identities through our language. In dialects there are more differences than just whether or not someone pronounces r, of course.

Accent refers to the way we pronounce words. Everyone has an accent and accents vary according to where we are from, who we are talking to, and when you learned the language you are speaking. In some dialects, for example, people say *dis* and *dat* for *this* and *that*. Actors mimic this practice to produce a unique character, and people who speak English natively can readily imagine the stereotypes this accent points to.

One recognizable social dialect in the United States is African-American Vernacular English (AAVE), also called Black English or Ebonics. Because of its high profile in rap and hip hop, it provides a useful case of dialects with prestige in some situations and not others. In response to a crisis in the education of young African-Americans, the sociolinguist William Labov (1981) published a pamphlet on this dialect called *The Study of Nonstandard English*. In it he reported on a large study of what we now call AAVE, and wrote the grammatical rules people were using. His stated goal was to help teachers and other educators understand their students' variety of English. The effect of this publication is much larger, however. Labov shows in great detail that AAVE is not merely slang and it is not ungrammatical or bad English. It is a language with grammatical rules. The fact that we call it a dialect means only that another dialect of English has been chosen to be the written standard.

## THE SYMBOLIC POWER OF LANGUAGE

The notion that Standard English is more correct, and therefore more valued, is actually based on which speakers have the most power in US society. In 1945, a linguist, Max Weinreich famously summarized the situation when he said that a language is a dialect with an army and a navy. He meant that those in power determine which dialect will be the one used in government, courts, business, and schools. In any country where different dialects are spoken, the one that is considered to be correct or better than the others is the language of the most powerful people. This power is usually social, economic, and political. In some cases, of course, war was a reality. It is no accident that a southern dialect did not become the standard in the United States. Although there are regional dialects and social ones, such as AAVE, the unspoken assumption in schools and universities is that only mainstream English is appropriate in the classroom.

In terms of consequences to our students in seminar, just as important as a belief in linguistic ideology is the reproduction of this ideology in our educational system, which occurs daily. Pierre Bourdieu (1991) has explained this process as the linguistic marketplace. He points out that those who defend a standard language as having value ignore the fact that it only has value based on the marketplace. One way of envisioning this marketplace is to think about Global English. English is the medium of instruction in universities in Hong Kong, Singapore, India, Pakistan, and increasingly in France and many other countries. It is the language of international business as well. Those who know English can get better jobs, and so its value is high around the world. In the case of Standard English, this marketplace is dynamic and contested. Standard English has symbolic value because it is perceived as being more correct than other varieties. That symbolic power is reproduced throughout the academic world, where teachers and professors are hired if they are perceived to speak and write this variety of English, even though, as we have seen, it would be better to label that language mainstream English. Those hired in turn serve on hiring committees and hire those who speak and write as they do. They order textbooks to teach this variety and help keep the book production in countries where writers and those working in book companies speak English as a native language. The marketplace thus perpetuates the power of those who control the symbolically valued language.

The people directing educational policy in the United States at federal, state, and local levels have argued successfully that all students need to learn Standard English so they can move beyond their neighborhoods, be more successful in school, and get jobs. The power of determining which dialect will be taught in schools is being contested by linguists advocating for social change. Some researchers argue that using a student-centered approach in the classroom and using the students' language, such as AAVE, may be more important to learning than focusing exclusively on Academic English (Alim & Baugh, 2007). They consider this an issue of language rights.

Language rights are important to consider in seminar. Students may speak a wide variety of dialects or styles, and even though these may not be prestigious in terms of college study, they have prestige among students for a variety of reasons. If the majority of the students in your classes speak a dialect outside of class, using it in class can have high prestige. It is the language of the area, or the language of a social group that has local power. Unlike many students, faculty members often do not share the same social and economic and geographic backgrounds as their students. We cannot assume that we all hold the same values about language or ways of talking. My practice is to ask when I don't understand an idiom or turn of phrase. The students love to explain what they mean, whether it has to do with the local vernacular, current slang, video games, or television.

Academic discourse is similar to Standard English, with the noted addition of specialized terminology from various disciplines. Few will dispute that in college, learning and using Academic discourse is important and students need to learn to use it in order to read required texts, understand lectures, and write essays. In my teaching, I encourage students to use mainstream English and the terminology they are learning in their speaking and writing. Academic discourse is not a dialect of English, but we can talk about various disciplines as having a register. Registers are ways of talking among groups of people who are engaged in the same activities. Academics use terminology specific to their disciplines and so do professional athletes and mechanics and soldiers and parents. In this book I am not using much linguistic terminology because specialized registers, while useful to speakers in the same discourse community, are hard to understand for outsiders. Sometimes we need to learn part of a register, such as when we order a coffee from a barista. What is important about all of these varieties of English (or any language) is that we understand that we need to speak differently in different situations, and that we already do. It is not a huge cognitive demand to learn new registers. We do this all of the time.

One of my students writes about academic discourse for an exercise in an interdisciplinary class, Evolving Communication, that I co-taught with an evolutionary biologist:

In seminar it is frequently the case that those who are more knowledgeable use advanced terms or descriptions. An example from seminar earlier today was invaginate, which I'm still not sure I understand, as well as *I resonated with* rather than *I liked* or *I found particularly interesting*. It often appears that those who speak more confidently and/or use more sophisticated or scientifically detailed phrases obtain dominance over the discussion. This tends to sway those who prefer or tend to speak more causally, or aren't as confident in their ideas. I've noticed that even when those who use more common terms speak, their ideas can frequently be overlooked and restated later by those who speak in more advanced, scientific vocabulary, unless they confidently insert themselves into the discussion repeatedly. In other words, when a quiet person pipes up to make one point, however significant, it isn't always retained by others unless they speak confidently and with "big words" or at least with a degree of eloquence.

This student points out the power of language that is multisyllabic and eloquent —it is more persuasive. If a student is unable or unwilling to speak this way, then, they risk not being heard or having their ideas attributed to others who can state them in the prestige variety—academic discourse.

Besides learning to use academic discourse, understanding the symbolic nature of language use is crucial. Not only do we each select certain ways of expressing ourselves, we can be classified by the language we use. Many students are quite aware of this point if they are unaccustomed to academic discourse or if they speak differently than most of the other students because of regional, social, or class differences. A researcher who worked with first year students of color reported that a Latina student, Maria, knew how to "talk like they [teachers and other students] expect me to," but she chose not to. From her point of view, using this discourse was using "big words," and this was the same as "acting white" and "selling out." Maria also complained about other students of color: "it's like they try to be like them [the White students] so that they'll like them, so they'll fit in" (White, 2011, p. 259).

## USING "LIKE"

If we hear ideas phrased in mainstream English and the terminology we have been teaching, do the ideas resonate more? It is important to reflect on this point. If students use informal English or a dialect, they are doing so in part to signal solidarity and their own identities. They may not have fluency in mainstream English. One use of language that points to informality and, for some faculty, unclear thinking, is the liberal use of "like." In (4), two students use "like." I've italicized them to make the many instances visually clear to the reader.

(4)

Sarah: How are we defining gender or *like* what does social influence mean in terms of sex versus gender and *like* male versus female talk?

Ashley: Well, I think I think sex is *like* absolute. *Like* you can determine physically

Sarah: [ok

Ashley: you are this sex. But I think *like* for me– the way I understood what Susan was saying– gender is *like* society's idea of male. And society's idea of female. And so you've got *like* this whole set of criteria whereas with sex it's physical. But with society it's *like* all these emotional things and then you can't say you're exactly one or exactly the other because there's *like* a whole range. Whereas *like* with physical characteristics you either have it or you don't.

**45**

*Candace*: Yeah you can— you can be all male— or you can be all male and all female but you can't be completely masculine or completely feminine. Is that—

*Many*: yeah

*Jessica*: That's— that's what I thought.

*Leah*: That's what a continuum means.

Sarah says in the first line, "or *like* what does social influence mean." Like introduces a rephrasing of her first question (*How are we defining gender?*). It is equivalent to "I mean." Sarah's next use of like, "and *like* male versus female talk" highlights the contrasting terms she wants to discuss. Researchers have found that this one word has multiple meanings and it can only be placed in certain parts of a sentence. Although it may seem to be sprinkled about, the use of like has rules. There are at least two additional uses of like (not found in the example): the first is its use as a synonym for *about*, used before numbers: *It was like 10 miles away*. This is very common and not restricted to adolescents or 20-somethings. The second is its use to quote what someone else said or thought: *She was like, are you sure?* It is reported speech. Linguists have researched syntactic changes involving slang, or colloquial ways of talking. *Like* is attested since the nineteenth century in England, but it is now more heavily used and stigmatized. Research indicates that children around the age of 10 begin using it, and it becomes less frequent in age groups of 30 and above (Tagliamonte, 2005) in informal talk.

Even though students may be using a particular variety of English that is not considered academic discourse, they may be contributing usefully to the learning. Note that Ashley uses "whereas," an academic term not usually heard in informal conversations. She structures her response by defining sex briefly, then gender in more detail, and then she returns to define sex to contrast what she has just said. She also indicates how she knows what she is saying. She uses "I think" and "the way I understood what Susan was saying" as ways to position herself as an authority even though she does not use academic terminology. This is a well-structured response in terms of contrasting definitions. The three students who speak after her ratify it as a clear response because they do not question her; instead, two of them agree. Using *like* does not automatically signal incoherent thought.

In order to hear what students are saying, we can focus on what is evoked in the language they are using. Here Sarah is confused about terms and Ashley compares and contrasts them referring to the definitions presented in the lecture. Being able to explain concepts is the best way to learn them, and this collaborative effort indicates learning is underway. As in academic writing, the key features of the conversation here are adopting a voice of authority, "the way I understood what Susan was saying"; using the discipline-specific vocabulary such as "continuum"; and providing evidence "all these emotional things."

## USING ACADEMIC DISCOURSE

In a seminar examining the oil industry, students use mostly academic discourse as they disagree about the purpose of business. Trevor analyzes the discussion of profits in the text on a particular page and concludes that the purpose of business is not just to make profits but to make a better life, a point that counters what Jennifer had just said—that the sole purpose of business is to make profits. He next asks her a direct question in (5):

(5)

Trevor:  Then I would ask you ( ) if the purpose of business is to make a good life and corporations are the biggest form of business then is it really wrong to make corporation– like give corporations more rights?

Jennifer:  Well I guess

Trevor:  =if– if they're doing good. I'm sorry.

Jennifer:  Is it

Trevor:  = Don't you want to protect them or like say another corporation might be just ( )

Jennifer:  Yes I think you do. But I think that the problem with them having so many rights is that they take on this life of their own. Where profit becomes simply a dollar amount like that's expressed in the ( ). This is our profit and it doesn't measure the pollution they put out it doesn't measure the people they made sick it doesn't measure the– you know all this stuff that is significant as far as making life. And and then my question for you would be is– are corporations really fulfilling on that thing of making life

Trevor frames an if-then statement (used in logic) as a question by prefacing it with "I would ask you." Phrasing the question this way presents a disagreement in an impersonal way. Jennifer responds at the end of the transcript "and then my question for you would be." She uses a similar phrasing with the use of "would." In Jennifer's response, she tries to present three things that the company does not measure, and three is a common number in presenting evidence persuasively. The way she repeats "it doesn't measure" is also used in academic writing and is called parallel structure; in addition, that repetition is effective. In rhetoric it is anaphora.

In (5) another aspect of academic discourse is revealed—remaining dispassionate. Jennifer and Trevor gain authority in seminar through the language they use and over time, they could gain power if their ideas remain useful and relevant. That power would allow them to speak longer and more often. This gives students power because they control the agenda and reduce the amount of time others have to respond.

**47**

## USING EMOTION

Their dispassionate approach is in contrast to (6) where Dan presents an emotional approach through his words and gestures. He is rather inarticulate because of his many pauses and he waves the book as he is speaking as a nonverbal way of referring to the author. FM means faculty member.

> (6)
>
> *Dan*: Now I haven't *bought* her pancake mix and I haven't bought her pancake syrup er er maple syrup but (.) I'm– I'm no more responsible for (1) for her racism (.) symbol than (.) he is. ((holding up the book)) and I– and I– and I don't (.) *own* his (1) um (2) ((hits book on the table)) I just really take issue with the whole idea that we white Americans are responsible for perpetrating this. racist. symbol. because it's still on the shelf. ((shrugs)) so
>
> *Ian*: but– but if ( )
>
> *Dan* [so so but see it's been *changed* ((much louder and large arm gestures in the air)) so that so that the edges are smooth (.) they don't know (.) diddly about it do we
>
> *FM*: But isn't that sort of the point of the book.

After this exchange the faculty member, another student, and Dan continue the conversation, but it is clear that Dan has not understood the author's argument and that he is choosing to disagree with it from a personal and emotional standpoint ("I'm no more responsible for– for her racism symbol than he is," and "we white Americans"). He holds the floor for about five minutes and this gives him a measure of power because his comments provide the agenda during that time. On the other hand, because he approaches the text from his personal habits as a consumer, he does not gain authority as a critical thinker.

## RESISTING AUTHORITY

Not all student comments actually promote collaborative learning, of course. Some divert attention from the topic. In (7) a student in a literature class diverts attention from the work. The faculty member (FM) is male and he noted that Greg's "why" challenged his authority and the necessity of doing the required work (Bergvall & Remlinger, 1996, p. 466).

> (7)
>
> *Scott*: I probably had to read the story about twelve times (just to get ahold of it)
>
> *Greg*: That's why it's so short.

| | |
|---|---|
| *Class*: | ((laughter)) |
| *FM*: | That's what careful reading is all about. Some people just do it for enjoyment and with something like this you probably want to look at it more than once. |
| *Greg*: | [well I don't. I couldn't see myself reading that more than once. ((loudly)) |
| *Class*: | ((loud laughter)) |
| *FM*: | You didn't like it that's all. That happens |
| *Greg*: | [I know |
| *FM*: | But to do a journal entry you probably have to read it more carefully than that even if you don't like it. |
| *Greg*: | =Why? |
| *Veronica*: | Because he sa:ys so: ((lengthens vowels and uses creaky voice, laughing)) |
| *FM*: | Well just because you have to y'know make assignments for people who go to classes. It's not just a power trip. |

Greg's and Veronica's assertions momentarily divert attention away from analysis of the story and indicate a way to resist the authority of the faculty member. Resistance can come in many forms, and in this exchange it is through humor.

## CONCLUSION

Seminars are conversations where power shifts occur. Students who have developed a voice using critical thinking and who have learned ways of speaking that gain the attention of others have more power, and faculty members who facilitate seminars sometimes reinforce those voices. Others can challenge that power, as we have seen in (7). It is important to remember that power is connected to ideologies. Students can find that another student's perspectives are powerful because they draw on local identities such as family and friends in the neighborhood, or popular identities such as musicians, athletes, or actors. These identities are tied to ideologies about how and when to speak, style and word choice. As Foucault (1972) points out, there are always multiple ideologies at play and they are produced and reproduced through discourse. Unless you become attuned to the ways students talk informally, you may not notice the power some students have. I had a student recently who was very comfortable talking at length. I noticed that students looked up to him because of his verbal facility. I, on the other hand, often asked him to relate his comments to the text because he spoke in generalities relying on anecdotes from his own experience. Although his experience was related to our reading, I wanted to focus on particularities in the text. Possibly because of my own bias about the value of analyzing a text on its own merits, it took me a couple of weeks to recognize the power that this

**49**

student exerted. Because he had the respect of others, it was important that I guide him towards the critical reasoning I expected in seminar so that he would lead others in that effort.

Although specific terminology and rhetorical moves are important, what makes a seminar effective is serious inquiry. This means analyzing the text to discover patterns and how the parts fit together. In every discipline and every interdisciplinary class, we are looking for patterns, and that is at the heart of seminar. When students are focused on this activity, whether it is working on the definition of concepts as in (4), big questions such as the purpose of business in (5), or interpreting the author's thesis as in (6), they are engaged in academic inquiry. We know it is occurring when students are asking questions or making observations about the text that synthesize their own experiences, other texts, and other class materials. Even when students have not understood parts of the text, they are still learning how to test their understanding with others. These moves or activities are as important as the language students use.

## BEST PRACTICES

■ Explain aspects of academic discourse to your students. They can refer to the text by the author's last name. They can also use the terminology they're learning in class. I always encourage my students to do that and I explain that they are all budding linguists emphasizing our community of practice. In interdisciplinary classes, I always say that I will be a co-learner because I do not have deep expertise in all the texts we examine but I model using the terminology my colleagues introduce. Of course, most important to academic discourse is teaching students to analyze the text, but referring to concepts is part of that analysis.

■ Learning new roles of interaction is part of seminar learning. I have learned that asking students to identify their own role in seminar is hard for them to do; however, they are very good at identifying the roles of others. Below is a list of roles my students created in a brainstorming exercise in one of my classes. By doing this exercise in your class, students can reflect on their own role(s) and how they impact others. Here is our list:

— Shy people, the philosopher, the artist, the dominant talker, the person who always has an opinion, the talker whose comments are not relevant, active listeners, observers, geniuses, people who posture, people who bring in abstract topics (such as "what is reality?"), people who are oriented to their own religion, people who provide quotes from the book—relevant or not, people whose experience is unique, people who like to hear themselves talk, people who have to be asked to contribute, people with wide experience, people who ask for breaks, people with computers, people who ask a question with a question, false facilitators (no authority to be one), the person with a simple solution, the devil's advocate, the I don't know-ers, the naysayers, the brown-nosers, the sleepers, the absent ones, the knitters, the eaters, the victim, the eager beavers.

- You can also brainstorm to hear discoveries that students made about their seminar participation after two weeks of the term. Here is a partial list from one of my seminars:

  — I understand how the conversation can proceed and how the faculty interacts as part of the group.

  — Gender is not a simple binary of male/female, but many people make generalizations about the way gender influences conversation style.

  — I thought I had to make statements and now I know I can ask a question.

  — I can say I'm confused and usually someone else will nod.

  — I'm less quick to disagree. I try to think about different proposals first.

- It is useful to announce that seminars are not places where a consensus must be reached. In fact, if everyone is contributing, there can be lots of disagreement and unresolved questions. The key to an effective seminar is stating those disagreements respectfully and not being afraid to raise questions or question assumptions. If students leave seminar with lots of new questions, that is usually a good result.

- Consider asking big questions in your class, which students address several times over the term. In one of my recent team-taught, interdisciplinary classes, we asked two questions: How do campaigns and the media use language and numbers to persuade voters? Why is this important for how people participate in our democratic society? Students wrote an essay that they revised every two weeks on these questions. They produced solid analyses of their reading and many began to create their own syntheses. Students struggled with this assignment, but they appreciated tackling the relationship between voting, media campaigns, and democracy by drawing on what they were learning. We used peer editing for this assignment, providing a checklist for students to refer to. A final seminar on your big questions would provide an opportunity for students to hear each other's well-developed ideas.

# Chapter 4

# Improvisation and Performance

## The Importance of Timing

Conversation is a performance, improvised from the moment it begins. Although we may have a plan for what we want to tell someone and even how we want to do that, more often than not, our plans don't work out. That is because we are responding to the words and gestures of others in conversation with us, and not just acting on our own. We discuss our opinions, our schedules, and the events of the day without thinking much about how our conversations flow. And that flow depends on everyone in the conversation; in effect, when we talk, we are also participating in a musical ensemble. Unlike jazz, where improvisation has particular rules of repetition by each player in the ensemble, conversations are unpredictable in terms of the length and content of each person's turn. In seminars the performance aspect of conversation becomes apparent. In order to enter the conversation, we need to focus on our timing—it's not always easy to get a word in because there are many potential speakers. Also, once we have the floor, many of us become aware of the time we and others take in voicing ideas because of this performance aspect.

Conversational performances are similar to those in theater, dance, and musical ensembles because they are all rhythmically based performances. By that I mean that conversations fundamentally rely on the timing of each person's entrance on stage or into the piece. The coordination of conversational moves and gestures, and the effects of the dramatic or musical pause all reflect this reliance on time and timing. It turns out we speak on a tempo and unconsciously match the tempo of other speakers, at least briefly. This may be rather startling, and you may be thinking to yourself, how can that be true if I don't already know it? How do time and timing coordinate our performance in seminars?

## TAKING TURNS IN CONVERSATION

Let's consider a rather mundane fact. We sometimes begin speaking at the exact same moment as another person. And, we don't consider this perfect timing an extraordinary event. One reason is that it happens often enough that it does not seem unusual. Yet, it doesn't happen regularly or we wouldn't be able to talk easily to others. In fact, most of the time we take turns in conversation, and we become aware of that when two people begin to speak at the same moment. In seminars, it is fairly common for two people to begin to speak at the same time because not all students raise their hands to gain the floor. And, even if students look around the room to check whether others are beginning to speak, it is difficult to judge the right moment. Most of the time when two people begin speaking at the same time in this situation, one can just begin again, or one of the speakers signals that the other can proceed: *go ahead*. And, there can be more negotiation, of course. This is such a brief and common occurrence, that it does not usually cause trouble in the conversation. Interruptions, however, can be problematic.

In (1), Jack interrupts Ella, a soft-spoken student. She disagrees with him about his analysis of Frederick Taylor's methods of scientific management. Jack stated that Taylor was studying ergonomics to help workers do a better job and Ella suggests he was instead interested primarily in increasing workers' output.

(1)
1 *Ella*:  That was one of the things that I didn't care for about him (.)
2       because he *was* like a physiologist type– he's measuring
3       you know very brilliant and everything ((faster)) but he wasn't (.) to me coming
4       (.) at it from the aspect of ergonomics it was more (.) how much (1) labor can we
5       (1) pump out of these (2) ((gestures, laughs))
6 *Jack*:                              [I think he (indistinguishable)
7 *Ella*:  =workers (.) and not um (1) the *human* you know like
8       what is the effect on the human (.) bodies down the road.

Ella speaks quietly and her speech is choppy because she often pauses throughout her turn. In lines 4–5, she says *how much labor can we pump out of these* and then in the two second pause, she puts both her hands on the table and laughs. At that moment of laughter, Jack tries to enter the conversation, but Ella has not finished her phrase (*these workers*). Was Jack paying close attention to Ella? Why did he begin to take his turn while Ella was gesturing and before she finished her sentence? It could be that even though she seemed to be holding the floor with her arms stretched before her on the table, the pause was much longer than her other pauses, and he may have believed she was finished speaking. Another factor is that he did not agree with her point and wanted to get the floor again. The improvisation can be momentarily thrown off by another speaker coming in too soon. In this case, Ella completed her turn forcing Jack to wait and the tempo remained steady. Moments of interruption like (1) do not usually cause a problem in seminar. In this case, Jack has a chance to talk after Ella finished. If it happens more than once, students will notice that a student is more interested in sharing his ideas than listening carefully to others.

When turn taking goes smoothly, we are attuned to each other in a fundamental way: we choose a time to begin speaking that keeps the conversation going. Researchers have proposed several theories about how we choose this moment to speak. The first analysts noted that there is often a pause between turns. Pauses, however, can come at any moment in a turn, and the speaker may not be finished with a turn when pausing as we saw in (1). To resolve this problem, conversation analysts have shown that there are various possible moments in anyone's turn where another speaker might come in and these are after clauses, phrases, or words. By imagining each of these moments as possible transition moments, we see that there are single words or clusters of words that have meaning to the listener as a response, question, or statement. The listener often, but not always, waits for one of these phrases to end. Intonation can play role as well. If a speaker uses a falling intonation, as at the end of a sentence, or uses rising intonation in a question, these are cues that the next speaker can take a turn. Paying attention to these cues in a large group can be very difficult, so you may find it easier to ask students to raise their hands when they want to speak.

## CONVERSATIONAL SYNCHRONY

We also pay close attention to body movements and synchronize our movements with each other's speech (Condon & Ogsten, 1971; Condon 1976). The psychologists who study this phenomenon call it conversational synchrony. We move our bodies with our speech and we synchronize our talk with other speakers. In seminar students can mirror each other, so if one crosses their arms, another may do the same. In (2), a seminar on Marxism, Shannon is explaining the question she put on the board and she has her hands linked behind her head, elbows out. She raises her hands briefly as she provides two possible answers to her question keeping them intertwined. Several people voice agreement on the second possibility she raises, but only Isaac continues talking. When the camera moves to him we see that he is mirroring her by holding his hands linked behind his head, elbows out.

(2)

Shannon: ((two hands behind her head, elbows out)) well I wasn't sure if he was just referring specifically to economics or if he was talking about (1) he was being able to access their true nature↑ In the more they produce the less they're able to access that↑ or if it's strictly

**55**

economic like the more money you produce the poorer you become. Economically ((raises hands)). or both ((raises hands)) I mean I don't know

*Many*:     [I think it's both

*Isaac*:     =I saw it as both I was thinking but it's ((he mirrors Shannon's pose)) (2) I don't know I couldn't come up with it especially the economic part I mean was he

*Shannon*:   [right

*Isaac*:     talking about um (1) the worker becomes poorer

*Shannon*:               [((Shannon drops her arms))

*Isaac*:     in relation to the accumulation of capital?

Isaac actually begins to speak after several others and because the camera does not show him at that moment, we cannot be sure, but it is likely that he gets the floor because he mirrors Shannon's pose. She drops her arms when it is clear that he doesn't have an answer and she remains on tempo by timing that movement with his "um."

We're not always in sync. Most of us have experienced becoming suddenly aware of the passing of time in a conversation because we can't seem to get in sync with the person we're talking to. The conversation can seem jerky, and we don't feel much rapport with the other person. This sudden awareness means that in most other conversations we do manage to time our turns appropriately. In fact, speakers have styles of turn-taking that allow pauses of various lengths. Pause length is important to consider because some people expect a short pause between turns and others are uncomfortable with even the slightest pauses between turns. By slight pause, I mean pauses longer than 0.2 seconds, because pauses that are shorter are imperceptible to speakers and listeners (Tomason & Hopper, 1992). How can we imagine fractions of seconds? One method is to listen to the Bee Gees song, *Stayin' Alive*. A group of medical researchers used this song to help doctors improve their performance of CPR (cardiopulmonary resuscitation) by achieving at least 100 compressions per minute. (The song has 103 beats per minute.) The method worked, suggesting that we have mental metronomes that we can call up in particular moments (Hafner, Sturgell, Matlock, Bockewitz, & Barker, 2012).

Besides pauses, we listen for a tempo in our conversations. Research by phoneticians using computers indicates that for native English speakers, there is a particular rhythmic pattern when one speaker ends a turn and another begins: the last two stressed syllables of the speaker's turn are used by the next speaker to continue the tempo. This is so common that when it does not occur, usually by coming in a little late, then speakers take note in some way. We might wonder if the person coming in late is hiding something. In other instances clarification occurs (Couper-Kuhlen, 1993). By clarification, I mean that speakers use a wide number of strategies to make sure they and their listeners are clear about the topic or, in telephone conversations, to find out if the other person is still on the line. Examples of these could be *so you're saying* or *Are you still there?*

## THE TEMPO OF TALK

Tempo is present in all our conversations, helping us to take turns and to begin to speak at the exact same moment as someone else. As I mentioned earlier, researchers have found that we actually synchronize our movements and gestures with other speakers in a sort of conversational synchrony. In fact, infants just four months old synchronize their body movements rhythmically with the speech of adults, both caregivers and strangers (Jaffe et al., 2001). Other researchers have found that in conversations, listeners time their movements rhythmically with the speaker's tempo of speech (Erickson & Shultz, 1982; Fiksdal, 1990). In (2), Shannon raises her hands on the important words of her two answers "economically" and "both," which indicates synchronous timing.

By looking at tempo in various languages, researchers have established the importance of the stressed syllable when a speaker takes a turn. English speakers regularly match the previous speaker's tempo at that moment (Couper-Kuhlen, 1993). English is a stress-timed language, and stressed syllables fall on the beat. We can hear stressed syllables in the conversations around us, and the stress can change the meaning of an utterance. If I say, "I have *TEN* marbles" I indicate that the number of marbles matters in the conversation. If I say "I have ten *MAR*bles" then the marbles matter more than the number. In contrast, Cantonese is a syllable-timed language, so stress is not a factor in distinguishing meaning. Like speakers of romance languages such as French, speakers of Cantonese pronounce their syllables with nearly equal stress rather than varying it. Still, in one study when speakers of Cantonese or other syllable-timed languages spoke English, they perceived and matched the tempo of a native English speaker at the turn transition (Reed, 2010).

Rhythm in talk is actually not very unusual. Hip hop and rap music relies on a rhythm, and some songs resemble talk. In poetry, there is a rhythm that is established by the meter. Each pair of unstressed and stressed syllables makes up a unit called a foot. In Emily Dickenson's well known poem, "Because I Could Not Stop for Death," I place a slanted line (/) after each foot and I use italics for the stressed syllables. (Stress in a syllable is a combination of loudness, pitch, and duration.)

Be*cause*/ I *could*/ not *stop*/ for *death*/ ,
He *kind*/ly *stopped*/ for *me*/ .

It turns out that just as in rhymed poems, in conversations we time our stressed syllables so that they are fairly evenly spaced. Limericks are a useful way to think about this because their structure causes us to emphasize or stress a syllable that normally would not be stressed to maintain the rhythm. In our conversations, we make use of the same features poetry does and we time our speech according to an underlying tempo. You can almost use a metronome to mark it, but it is not quite that regular. To hear this tempo for yourself, listen to talk radio or a television program with conversations, and then listen not to the content of what people are saying, but the stressed syllables. Once you have adjusted your listening, begin tapping out the beat you're hearing with the stressed syllables. Using your hand or foot will help you do this. You may begin to hear the underlying tempo.

Here is a brief, invented conversation with these features highlighted. I have italicized the stressed syllables and used the same foot structure as in the poem so you can hear the stressed beats if you read it out loud. Unlike Dickenson's poetry, in conversations we can squeeze several words between stressed syllables and we can slow down our rate of speech to make each syllable fall on the beat. Try to read this conversation like the poem so that it has a regular beat. Begin by tapping out the beat and then time your reading accordingly.

Q:    I didn't know *what*/ in the world he was *say*ing/.
       I mean *two*/ and *two*/ are *four*/.
Z:    *Oh*/ I know what you *mean*/.

Sometimes in conversations no words fall on the beat, but the beat does not disappear because we're using it to time our pauses as well. If you are watching speakers in a conversation, you will see that their gestures, no matter how slight, are also on tempo as in (2). Amazingly, even when there is a pause of several seconds, speakers still come in on the beat.

## RATE OF SPEECH

There are other rhythmic structures in conversation, such as speech rate. The number of words between the beats varies because speech rate is a resource we all use to convey various effects. The comic, Groucho Marx, is famous for talking really fast, but if you listen for the tempo in one of his movies, you'll hear that it remains steady even though he can say far more words between the beats than other characters. You may notice that speakers do not all speak at the same rate in your experiments in listening for tempo. Rate of speech can be exploited for various effects; for example, a speaker that wants to emphasize talk that has higher relevance may use fewer words between beats than the talk before and after. Many of us make use of this in lectures. Slight tangents such as parentheticals, afterthoughts, and summaries may have a quicker rate of speech as well (Uhmann, 1992). In (1) above, Ella temporarily speeds up her rate of speech when she says, *you know very brilliant and everything* to acknowledge the positive traits of an author before elaborating on the negative ones. By speeding up, she creates a parenthetical space in her talk. Whether speaking with a fast or a slow rate in terms of numbers of words between the beat, speakers maintain the tempo in a conversation.

Pavlenko (2005) summarizes research on vocal cues signaling emotion with speech rate. In English, we signal excitement and anger with a fast speech rate and timidity, shame, and confidence with a low speech rate. In seminar, it can be useful to listen for speech rate to gauge the emotion students are bringing to their ideas. If they are emotionally engaged, they are less likely to listen carefully to other students and good points can be lost. I will sometimes call for a pause for reflection if I feel the conversation is too emotional.

## HIGH-CONSIDERATENESS STYLE

Much of our awareness of language and linguistic practices such as tempo are unconscious, and we notice small disruptions to the flow of conversation when speakers don't follow the conventions we use. Many people believe that interrupting another speaker is a problem and I often hear of seminar rules listing prohibitions such as, *let each person speak*, *don't interrupt*, *one mic (microphone)*. But as we have seen, pauses can signal the end of a turn and they can also signal that the speaker is thinking and is not ready to give up the floor. Other speakers can misinterpret when to come into the conversation without meaning to interrupt. A preference for not interrupting usually indicates a conversational style—"high-considerateness." In High-Considerateness Style, speakers wait about half a second before taking a turn. This may not happen all of the time in every conversation, but it is a general conversational practice, and speakers with High-Considerateness Style not only use the pause but expect the turn taking to be the same with anyone who interacts with them. If another person begins talking at the same time, they may feel interrupted. This is an unconscious preference, and only when it is violated repeatedly do we take note of it.

## HIGH-INVOLVEMENT STYLE

Interrupting is a topic that was extensively studied by discourse analysts studying gender in the 1970s and 1980s because it seemed to be a way of asserting dominance in a conversation, but some began to question whether or not interruptions were always displays of dominance or power. Sociolinguist Deborah

Tannen (1981), for example, showed that what some speakers identify as interruption may actually be better explained as "overlapping." She audiotaped a conversation at a Thanksgiving dinner where she found some speakers often enthusiastically broke in while others were still talking. Even though the overlapping speech was on the same topic, during playbacks of the audiotape, she discovered that other speakers heard this as interruption and stopped talking. On the other hand, those who regularly overlapped other speakers felt that this style of turn taking indicated rapport and interest. They felt pauses in the conversation signaled a problem.

Overlapping, or taking a turn while another speaker is talking, is part of a High-Involvement Style that shows rapport. Tannen identified several guests including herself as using New York Jewish style at this Thanksgiving dinner, a High-Involvement Style. My students have pointed out that large families, particularly Italian ones, use this High-Involvement Style as well. The overlapper is indicating agreement and rapport by extending the topic. Interruption, in contrast, changes the topic. Regardless of intention, if a high-considerateness speaker is repeatedly overlapped by a high-involvement speaker, the resulting conversation is imbalanced, and the high-considerateness speaker can feel interrupted.

There are other styles besides high-involvement and high-considerateness involving pause length between turns. Researchers examining the speaking style of Athabaskans, a Native American tribe in Alaska, point out that they allow a long pause in turn-taking; in fact, they are very comfortable sitting together in silence—conversation is not necessary when visiting (Scollon & Scollon 1981). Their conversations include little or no overlap. The opposite occurs in the speech of rural Antiguans. Reisman (1974) describes conversations there as involving multiple voices at the same time, and if a new person enters the conversation, there is a brief, obligatory greeting but no other signal that anyone is ready to listen. Speakers can have their topics acknowledged or ignored, and that may or may not stop them from talking.

In mixed gender groups, speakers may use one style and then change that style in single gender groups. Two of the seminars I recorded were divided by gender for about 30 minutes before the groups came together to continue the conversation. In both smaller groups, some of the women overlapped each other extensively, but they did not do this in the larger group. The men used High-Considerateness Style in both settings. Expected pause length, then, may be quite different in different regional and ethnic settings and the same speakers may change their styles depending on the gender of other speakers.

## HIGH-INVOLVEMENT AND HIGH-CONSIDERATENESS STYLES IN SEMINAR

To illustrate High-Involvement and High-Considerateness Styles in a seminar context, I provide two examples that illustrate the definitions I provided above.

In (3) the three female students—April, Kirsten, and Lana—are in the middle of a heated conversation about Latino gangs in Los Angeles and April suggests using an inclusive pronoun, "our" rather than the exclusionary "their" that Kirsten has been using. April has the floor and then Lana joins April, who is trying to explain why the group should say "this country" rather than "our country." The speech is very rapid.

(3)
| | | |
|---|---|---|
| 1 | *April*: | Maybe we should be saying assimilate into *this* country |
| 2 | | Instead of *our* country. |
| 3 | *Kirsten*: | =Right excuse me. |
| 4 | *April*: | [I mean that's a big part of the problem |
| 5 | *April*: | is that there's so much talk about *our* country. |
| 6 | *Lana*: | [yeah |
| 7 | *April*: | This is (2) their (1) and this is |
| 8 | *Lana*: | =This is every one's |
| 9 | *April*: | This is *a* country |
| 10 | *Lana*: | everyone |
| 11 | *April*: | and the people in it (1) that I mean that's– that's– that's one of the [biggest problems here. |
| 12 | *Lana*: | [yeah |
| 13 | *Lana*: | =Is that we yeah you know |
| 14 | *April*: | =Is that we keep saying [*our* country. |
| 15 | *Lana*: | [our country. Whose country is it you know? |
| 16 | *April*: | =So– so– so why should *they* assimilate to *our* country |
| 17 | *Lana*: | [not feel integrated |
| 18 | *April*: | does our country (indistinguishable)? |
| 19 | *Lana*: | [(indistinguishable) to *our* country you know |

In our playback of the videotaped seminar, I asked April, who was using a High-Considerateness Style, what she was thinking when Lana joined in with her explanation of *our country*. Because she was somewhat tongue tied, as can be noted in lines 7 and 11 with her pauses and word searches, April said she welcomed Lana's help. Lana explained that she was showing support for April, and agreement. Her extended agreement included the *yeah* in line 13, and her attempts to finish April's thought in lines 16 and 19. In this case, even though the conversation was passionate, showing respect did not mean waiting for another speaker to finish her thought. Instead, sharing the floor was considered useful by April, a high-considerateness speaker, and usual by Lana, a high-involvement speaker. Lana continues her overlap so that it is hard to hear what either of them is saying, but it is clear that they are in agreement.

High-Considerateness Style has little overlap. A typical overlap in this style may be a listener's response to a speaker, such as "uh huh" or "yeah." This is different from the High-Involvement Style in which the overlap can be a phrase or more. In (4), students do not overlap, but the faculty member (FM) does at one point:

(4)

| | |
|---|---|
| *Anna:* | There's power in numbers (0.5) you alone it's *hard* to make a difference but (0.5) I agree with you. Educating those people a*round* you and then go on from there. ((quietly)) |
| *Leslie:* | And there's also responsibility in *know*ledge though. Then you're really– you're *stuck* then. (1) Cuz once you *know* something then (0.5) well (.) do you have to *do* [something] about it? |
| *FM:* | [yeah ((very quietly—the rest of her comment is indistinguishable)) |
| *Mick:* | [Yeah |
| *Mick:* | yeah I think that's *everyone's* predicament when they get into college kind of.<br>(1)<br>((Group laughter)) |
| *Mick:* | [So (1) at least that seems to be *mine* but (0.5) how much *can* I do (.) what *should* I do |
| *Anna:* | (1.5) So if people *were* more educated. (0.5) in issues such as (.) the one Dubois brings up. (1.0) would the p– would America be different now? |

Mick overlaps the faculty member in his first turn with his first "yeah" but then he waits before continuing to speak. These speakers use High-Considerateness Style. I include the timed pauses to show that their speech is also halting rather than fluent. Leslie and Mick are clearly thinking about what gaining knowledge might mean for them personally in terms of social activism. Anna's last question moves back to the text.

What is remarkable about these very brief interchanges is that turn taking is accomplished so that the speakers have no confusion about what each other has said, and even though the conversation is negotiated moment by moment, the speakers seem unaware of the subtle work they are doing in timing their entry into the conversation. In these seminars and in ordinary conversation, our turn taking is actually a very highly orchestrated endeavor. We need to negotiate moment by moment when we speak, introduce a new topic, agree, or disagree. In seminar, with many potential speakers, it is even more complicated for those with a High-Considerateness Style. They are waiting for a pause before they enter the conversation, but the pause may not occur at an appropriate moment for their remark. The topic may have changed, or moved in a different direction. That is why it is important to create pauses in the conversation. Even a brief break can be useful for students to reflect more on where the conversation is going.

## RECOGNIZING TEMPO

If we examine video tapes of conversation to further examine the notion of smooth and not so smooth interactions, we find parallels between what is going on in the conversation and in the tempo. In my research on interviews between academic advisors and Chinese students in a university, I found that advisors sometimes gave an explanation and then explained a point in that explanation further, giving a hyperexplanation. The hyperexplanation defined a point that did not really need defining given the situation. Advisors temporarily sped up their tempo when doing that. Unconsciously they may have realized that this part of their explanation was already understood so they could rush over it. In addition, I found that there could be tempo tugs, or very slight changes in tempo, reflecting an uncomfortable moment (Fiksdal, 1990). These changes were momentary, lasting a few seconds at best. They are not the result of conscious decisions, but they give additional information to the listeners about our meaning. Generally speaking, arrhythmia in our speech indicates a disruption in the talk.

This research indicates that there is a universal capacity for recognizing and adapting to a particular speaker's tempo. And, continuing the tempo allows for rhythmic integration of the each speaker's turn. Unlike these advising sessions, where advisors are attuned to listening for when students want to talk, seminars can pose a problem for nonnative speakers of English. They often do not have time to formulate what they want to say in time to enter the conversation. I address this point in Chapter 8 and Chapter 9.

## CONCLUSION

The notion of unconsciously establishing a tempo during ordinary conversation does not seem far-fetched if we think about the presence of music in our lives. Music and dance, which rely on rhythm, are universal—practiced in all cultures and for as long as history has been recorded. The concepts for music and dance may not be equivalent to our words "music" or "dance" but they are present (Turino, 2008). In Balinese, for example, music is referred to as "tradition" (Sean Williams, personal communication). Rhythms may not be organized in the same way in various cultures, but they exist across many performance-related activities. Anthropologists have suggested that the arts are central to human evolution because they provide a way to realize a collective identity, a part of a community. The shared knowledge of the performance structures is crucial to this realization, but so is the synchrony of moving and sounding together. Improvisational performances in seminars based on time and timing are fairly complex when we analyze them, and they rely on subtle cues that we are unaware of most of the time. Even though there may be disagreements, uncomfortable moments, and long pauses, the improvisation is based on an underlying tempo, so in this way we are always together in a collective performance. Tempo, then, is a fundamental organizing principle underlying all conversations and we become aware of it when we begin to speak at the same time, or have difficulty getting the floor.

## BEST PRACTICES

- Explain the fine-tuned performance that we create when we have seminar to your students. If they realize that they are already in an ensemble by virtue of the fact that a seminar conversation is based on a shared tempo, then they will be more open to the notion of collaborative learning. We are already collaborating at a micro level, and we sense disruptions to the rhythmic organization even if we cannot always be consciously aware of them.

- In your first seminar discuss how speakers will be recognized. I have found that some students quickly learn to scan the group before talking, and others do not. There are nonverbal indicators you can give to your students: while looking at the current speaker, the student may lean forward, raise a finger or hand slightly, and/or open their mouths to speak. You can also agree that students will raise their hands to speak. If students cannot see each other well, explain that they can listen for brief pauses and falling intonation, such as at the end of a written sentence. I ask that students not keep their hands raised for a long time as it is distracting for everyone. As facilitators, we can also take note of who wants to speak and call on them.

- One of the features of seminar is that speakers overlap each other and negotiate turns to speak (Gibson, Hall, & Callery, 2006). You can advise students that if they have something to say and were unsuccessful in getting a turn, they can find a way to interject it by listening for a related topic or waiting for a pause in the conversation. If the conversation has moved on, they can use one of the following phrases: *I would like to return to [the topic of], I had something to add a few minutes ago and I still think it's relevant,* or *Going back to what [Marilyn] said.* It is important for students to realize that topics can change rapidly, and if they have more to add to a particular topic, it is usually very useful for the group to go back to it. This can deepen the conversation in useful ways and other students will no doubt have more to add as well.

- Because interruptions are changes in topic, I believe it is important for a facilitator to point out when they occur, particularly when the interrupter does this repeatedly.

I usually do this immediately, sometimes interrupting the interrupter. In my experience, interrupters always excuse themselves quickly and yield the floor. Even if the previous speaker no longer wishes to speak, my move signals that interruptions should not occur. If you prefer not to intervene immediately, it is good practice to point out what happened at the end of the seminar so all students can improve their interactions and the seminar rules are upheld. In either approach, it is best to make general statements about interruptions rather than singling out students.

- High-involvement speakers like to fill pauses, so they often talk more than other students. Explaining these styles to your students can be very helpful. When I explain these styles, I always tell the story of meeting my brother-in-law for the first time. He grew up in New York City and I am from the west coast. He asked question after question, and did not seem to listen to the answer, instead overlapping me with another question. In addition, each question seemed to be more personal than the last. I thought he was a little aggressive, like the New Yorker stereotype; in fact, however, as I studied more sociolinguistics, I found that he used High-Involvement Style. All of us use different styles depending on what sort of situation we're in and who we're talking to. We are usually able to adapt to new circumstances by shifting our style. When everyone is aware of these (and other styles introduced in other chapters), you can occasionally call for a pause or point out that only some students are speaking a lot, adding: *probably because of their High-Involvement Styles.* I try to point out behavior rather than focus on particular students in my facilitation comments.

- If you are a high-involvement speaker, then it is important to point that out to your seminar because your style will no doubt affect your facilitation. You also may unconsciously expect your students to conform to your style, and they may not be able or willing to do that. Research in K–12 classes shows that teachers wait less than a second for students to respond. Since your questions in seminar will often require some reflection, it is best to wait at least two to three seconds. This can seem like a long time if you are a high-involvement speaker, but in my experience the pause allows a useful response or insight.

- Are some seminars fast-paced and others slow-paced? In my experience teaching and analyzing videotaped seminars, it is possible for both to occur, but usually there is a mix. When I needed to choose 30 minutes of a two-hour seminar to use in playback sessions, I had no difficulty finding a segment in which many students talked and the topic was well developed, even if there were other segments that seemed slow. My sense is that when we are fully involved teaching our seminars, we don't notice a slow pace because we're busy thinking. I noticed this phenomenon with students as they watched their seminar in playback. Sometimes they remarked that the pace seemed slow, but at the time it did not because they were so engaged.

■ If the seminar seems slow-paced and you had hoped it would cover more ground, you can divide students into small groups with specific assignments, and then reconvene to hear what they discovered. When you reconvene, ask groups to report out briefly. You could write main points on the board or ask students to do that individually. Try to allow some time for discussion of these main points so that all seminar members feel informed. Another way to refocus is to call for a pause and ask students to write for three minutes about what they have learned. This allows students to collect their thoughts and reflect. A third approach is to ask students to create another question with the person sitting next to them. This helps students move away from the original plan and build on the conversation that has already occurred.

# Chapter 5

# Getting the Floor

Getting the floor is a major concern for students in seminars. Some students feel they can't get a word into the conversation; others ask, *why don't people comment on what I say?* Getting the floor in seminar is not only making a comment or asking a question; it is introducing a topic or a perspective that everyone attends to. Some students speak when they have a point to make and others find it difficult to get a word in. Unlike discussions where the faculty member nominates each speaker, seminars are often free-flowing so students need to find ways to introduce their ideas into that flow. Even if students raise their hands, they may not be able to contribute their ideas at an appropriate moment because of the comments of intervening speakers. And, if the topic changes, many feel they can no longer contribute their idea. In (1) a student summarized her approach to getting the floor as follows:

(1)
I know I have problems interrupting people or problems in seminars about when to talk and when not to talk and I usually end up saying nothing because I don't want to step on anybody's toes or interrupt people. So I just kind of sit there and unless there's a huge void of silence then I tend to just not say much of anything or I can't find the right *time* to present what my ideas are so [. . .]

In her statement the student makes two points that are central to understanding why getting the floor can be difficult. She says she cannot find the "right time" to present her ideas and that she does not want to interrupt. The "right time" for her is the void of silence. This metaphor suggests that she finds herself together with others in a big empty structureless space when they are not talking. At that point she feels more comfortable speaking. The second point this student makes of not wanting to interrupt can mean several things such as having a high-considerateness conversational style, not yet having a voice, being shy or introverted, rehearsing what she wants to say instead of listening, and/or being unprepared. As we have seen in Chapter 4, having a high-considerateness conversational style means that speakers expect a brief pause between turns of talk and if speakers are overlapping or not allowing others to contribute by controlling the topics, then style can be a factor.

Not yet having a voice means the student may not have gained solid critical thinking skills and the courage to voice original ideas or good questions. Introversion and shyness are not the same thing. Cain (2012) points out that shyness is fear of social disapproval while introversion is a preference for environments that are not overstimulating. Students with these traits may be able to express ideas only after considering them for a while, and because topics can change rapidly, by the time they are prepared to speak the right moment has passed. These two perspectives on getting the floor—the right time and pace—indicate that speakers are aware of the appropriate times to enter the conversation as well as the moment by moment tempo (Fiksdal, 1990).

## METAPHORS TO DESCRIBE SEMINAR

Being "shy" or "talkative" as some students characterize themselves, may be useful for describing a personal identity, but examining the metaphors that students use in describing their seminars reveals a more complex picture of how we understand seminar and what it might mean to get the floor. In the quote cited above, the student says she cannot find the "right time" to present her ideas. If she thinks of seminar as having a void at times, then it is a container that she needs to jump into. Entering the conversation to interject an idea might be difficult because there is no clear structure.

As we saw in Chapter 2, IDEAS ARE OBJECTS. Ideas can be *torn apart, put into words, pulled out of the air, on the tip of my tongue.* In these expressions, ideas can be torn, put, pulled, and placed. A very accessible book that explains the pervasiveness of metaphors in our conversations is Lakoff and Johnson's (1980) *Metaphors we live by*. In it the authors argue that we not only use metaphors in our everyday speech and writing, we actually think metaphorically. I was interested in testing this idea when I conducted a study on how students described seminars. Over the course of one year, I videotaped seminars and then asked students and faculty members to watch edited versions with me individually in playback sessions. I categorized the metaphors students used to describe seminars and found six categories: SEMINAR IS A JOURNEY, SEMINAR IS A BUILDING, SEMINAR IS A MACHINE, SEMINAR IS WAR, SEMINAR IS A CONTAINER, and SEMINAR IS A FLOW (Fiksdal, 2008).

## Seminar is a Journey

SEMINAR IS A JOURNEY is the metaphor most used by the students in my study. In (2) I provide examples, each from a different student:

(2)
- When others go off on tangents or get off the subject, then I go into my prosecutor mode.
- People lose sight of the goal and stray.
- I'm totally lost as to what's going on here 'cause they're all talking at the same time, you know.
- We ended up talking around it 'til we got it. We kept going back and forth with that.

Going off on tangents, straying, becoming lost, going back and forth are all metaphors relating to a journey where there is a path, a specific direction, and a goal or end-point. For these students, the structure of the journey is useful to describe the conversation in seminar. It is important to realize that using this metaphor does not mean every tangent poses a problem even though tangents bring out one student's "prosecutor mode." If questioned about tangents, students and faculty will admit it is difficult to know in advance if tangents will be useful, so they are not necessarily problematic. In this study individual students and I are discussing particular moments in a seminar, so the student may have a negative evaluation of a tangent at one point without meaning to imply that they are all bad. I also discovered that each student had different goals. This divergence in goals means that the path the conversation should take may be satisfying to some and dissatisfying to others. Expressing a goal for every seminar is very useful for students thinking of seminar as a journey because they seem to monitor the conversation in terms of reaching that goal.

## Seminar is a Building

In the metaphor SEMINAR IS A BUILDING, the trajectory of the conversation is vertical rather than the more horizontal JOURNEY metaphor as these examples in (3) from different students show:

(3)
- It is a place to build on my ideas.
- I build on what I already know.
- We're starting at a common base.
- We got more and more information built on each other, which was good.

**69**

This metaphor indicates that some students start at a common base and then build on each other's ideas. It is the second most common metaphor used. It suggests that students are connecting their ideas to previous ones and they can see a structure in the conversation. For these students, laying a solid foundation is important. Students may be best prepared to build on ideas if the group begins by discussing themes or the argument in a text.

## Seminar is a Machine

A different focus is created with the metaphor SEMINAR IS A MACHINE, where various actions seem to be salient. In (4) some of the metaphors used by different students are listed:

(4)
- Just the ideas were spinning so fast that day just really fast. It was really fun to watch it.
- I felt like I was pretty engaged in this seminar and then I definitely shift back because that exchange sort of ended and there was a shift in the conversation and I disengaged some at that point.
- I didn't want to be deprived of her input.
- I know how I would like seminar to be run.

The actions of spinning, shifting, and running help explain the ways a machine works. It needs input in order to function. These students are using a metaphor that is often used to describe students who are learning—they are engaged in the work. Students using this metaphor may be happiest when the conversation is humming with ideas and they not fully understand that they have a responsibility to keep it going just as everyone else does.

## Seminar is War

A metaphor that is less evident in my study, but still present, is SEMINAR IS WAR. In (5) I provide examples from different students:

(5)
- Sometimes I feel like I've been just assaulted in seminar and uh, you know, it'll be for expressing a controversial opinion.
- Sometimes I feel that there is an exclusive group of people dominating the discussion and that interrupting them might be combative.
- I don't feel like I learn much from him because he's mostly just trying to cut people down.
- [She] sometimes reinforces what I'm thinking and sometimes it challenges what I'm thinking and sometimes it just totally blows me away because I never thought of something from that focus.

In these metaphors students describe other students in a war-like setting: being assaulted, combative, and cutting people down. These comments do not indicate a good environment for learning. Nevertheless, the last statement about being reinforced, challenged, and blown away is a positive statement about the power of another student's ideas. Students who see seminar as war may need work on creating a strong voice in seminar so that they can help change seminar dynamics. If you notice that a student is cutting other people down, you might point out that there are more than two sides to an issue or that there is a larger issue at play. This move can diffuse the situation without pointing fingers. In Chapter 8, I present cross-cultural dynamics that could also be present if war is a dominant metaphor for a student.

## Seminar is a Container

The metaphor SEMINAR IS A CONTAINER means that students are interested in getting into the conversation, and getting something out of it. In (6) I provide examples from different students:

(6)
- I wonder how much he gets out of seminar and I don't think he gets much, 'cause he always seems to be arguing rather than learning.
- When it's a particularly good one, I come out and feel sort of energized intellectually.
- I think as a whole the group got a lot out of it.
- I wasn't into this discussion.
- There is no room for emotion.

The container has boundaries so that people can enter it and leave it. There is room for certain kinds of conversation and not others and it is possible to get ideas out of the container, but no room for emotion for at least one student. A container may not have much structure besides walls, so if this is a dominant metaphor for students, it would be useful for them to make a concept map. They could write down the question or comment that is under discussion and draw lines to the various ideas that others generate. These new ideas may, in turn, become the topic. This sort of mapping can help students see a structure in the conversation besides the broad contours and it helps them find a way to comment, either to refer back to an earlier idea or to anticipate possible directions for the conversation.

## Seminar is a Flow

The final metaphor students used was SEMINAR IS A FLOW. In (7) are examples from different students:

(7)
- I think those are really classic examples of adding on to a general idea that's already flowing through the group.
- It's kind of interesting that the whole conversation has drifted to the power issue.
- [Seminar] flowed pretty much all the way through.
- I'll find a point that I want to make and . . . I'll make like a little speech in my mind and then usually I miss the right point to jump in.

Students need to jump into the flow, or they miss the point to jump in. It seems important that the flow be steady for one student. I categorized the comment, "I miss the right point to jump in," as SEMINAR IS A FLOW rather than SEMINAR IS A CONTAINER, where one could also jump in. I decided that missing the right point would be more salient if ideas were flowing by than if they had no apparent structure to each other except being contained. If students see seminar as a flow, in order to talk they need to enter an on-going stream, and finding the right point to jump in can be difficult because they do not control the conversation—no one does.

This flow metaphor is very different from taking a path at the fork of a road in a journey because it is not possible to retrace one's steps and go back to the fork in the road. In addition, there is no structure such as a path, building, or a container where ideas can be placed and the field of competition or battle is not laid out. If ideas flow by, it means retrieving and storing ideas is harder. If students need to plan out or rehearse what they will say, then the right moment for their idea may pass and they have no control over that. For these students, it is useful to point out that a major goal of collaborative learning is gaining a voice and that requires agency rather than passivity. They may need to experiment with interjecting small comments at first because they do not disrupt the flow very much. As they become more comfortable with the group, they may realize that helping to direct the flow, at least occasionally, is important to their own intellectual development.

I have found that students and faculty can discover the metaphors they use to understand seminars by writing about how they interact. After writing for three to five minutes, we stop and identify metaphors. Not surprisingly, this writing can reveal we are using more than one metaphor for seminar and metaphors can change depending on particular seminars that the writer refers to. Discovering how we conceptualize seminars is particularly useful if we are facilitating them. Recognizing that participants may have different conceptions of the shape, moves, and goals of the conversation can help the facilitator be more aware of what is going on. It also helps seminar members to see why finding the "right time" to present one's ideas is not a simple task.

## METAPHOR AND THE RIGHT TIME TO TALK

If we think about how we get the floor in seminar, one important consideration has to do with reasons for talking in the first place. I asked freshmen in a team-taught course to answer the question, "How do you decide when to talk in seminar?" I categorized the metaphors in 68 written responses to this question. The majority of students (17) said they talked if they had a valuable idea, even if it was only worth two cents. Eleven students mentioned planning their ideas and having confidence in those ideas. Eight students reported talking if they felt strongly about an idea. Three students needed to have an idea or an interesting one, and two spoke if they felt someone was "way off." In addition, students mentioned that they would speak in response to a question, when they didn't understand, or when they agreed or disagreed.

A quarter of these students wrote that they talked if they had a valuable idea of some kind, and some wrote they would talk if they had an idea no one else had, which may indicate value in its uniqueness. Some specific comments are listed in (8):

(8)
- I feel like the group discussion will benefit from my input. I tend to step back, watch others to see where things go, then put in my two cents worth.
- I only talk if I feel I have something of value to add to the discussion.
- If I have a clear idea which I think sheds light on what is being talked about, that no one else has said.
- I decide when to talk in seminars based on when I have an idea I think no one else has yet stated or to clarify/reword others' statements.

Note that the ideas or comments can be added or put into the conversation and an idea can shed light on it. Light and clarity are common metaphors for understanding: *a light went off in my head*; *that's a murky area*. Some metaphors highlight the fact that ideas are held by the individual and offered to the group. These students are clearly able to track the ideas that have already been offered and to weigh the value of their contribution prior to voicing it. Students believing they have a valuable contribution do not mention having trouble getting into the conversation.

In the next largest category, students plan what they will say before they talk, and some of them need to have confidence in their ideas as well. Examples are in (9):

(9)
- Before I talk in seminar I usually know what I have to say. It will be all planned out. Then I will wait for a break in the conversation and say what I want, but it never seems to work out. My words drift from my head and I end up saying something dumb.

- I form a complete thought or argument and wait for the appropriate time to respond. Unfortunately I am finding it difficult to "break" into a conversation that is currently running and the topic is usually long gone before I knew what happened. Just this last Thursday's seminar one guy spoke for about half an hour arguing something I thought was very wrong. So I gathered my response, my heart was beating very fast, and I began to shake just a little. I knew it was time to interject; however [the faculty member] took up right where I was prepared to begin and that was that.
- I usually wait until I have something that I really want to say, and have thought about, and when something related to this comment comes up, I wait for a pause and say it. I do not usually think out loud or say things off the top of my head.
- I don't usually speak up until I have formulated in my head exactly what and how I want to say something. It is also important that I feel as though I have a good grasp of the material and the seminar up to that point.
- In seminar I usually decide to talk when I have at least somewhat thought out what I am going to say. I also have to feel confident enough with my ideas to say them aloud.

For some of these students, planning works well, but others don't feel they sound intelligent, or the topic disappears before they can address it. Waiting for the right time can involve physical pressure as in the student's comments about "last Thursday's seminar" when her heart was beating and she was shaking. These students can be reassured that quite often they will hear their idea expressed by someone else if they don't voice it. It is often the case that even ideas that are not clearly expressed are understood by at least some students because they are often willing to try to clarify it. These students can benefit from working in small groups where they feel more comfortable.

In the next largest category, feeling strongly about an idea was key to the students' decisions about when to talk. I list examples in (10):

(10)
- I'm on fire, angered, and wish to speak out immediately.
- I usually have some serious question or emotional feelings that I want to share with the group. Because I am so shy, I usually don't talk unless somebody brings up that particular subject [. . .] I won't speak unless the conversation gets really intense.
- I talk in seminar when someone says something that hits me or triggers something in my mind [. . .] I will probably agree or disagree strongly.

- I just speak when something someone has said has struck a chord. When something hits me deep down and I feel very strong about an issue.
- When something really strikes me deep down, and I feel strongly about an issue.

In these cases, students need to feel strongly about an issue before they speak. You can explain that seminar conversations are everyone's responsibility and the goal is not to hear them speak only when they are personally moved by an issue, but also to work on a dispassionate, analytic level sometimes. The overall goal is to contribute to collaborative learning no matter what the topic is.

Only three students identified themselves as talkative. One comment (11) was quite useful because it shows a reflection on the student's role in seminar and a newfound understanding that she can restrain herself more easily now:

(11)
Knowing that I have a natural tendency to dominate group conversations, I do my best to consider the value of my thoughts for the group before speaking. This hasn't always been the case, but after a year abroad of being unable to communicate my ideas with ease, I've learned that the rest of the world can indeed survive without being enlightened of my every thought.

These comments help us see that students have very different approaches to the moment when they want to talk in seminar. By reflecting on when they talk in seminars and comparing their reflections with other students, seminar groups will see a wide variety of approaches to talking. Those who are talking a great deal and have no trouble getting the floor can better understand why pauses are necessary for others who also may want to contribute.

## STYLE AND THE RIGHT TIME TO TALK

Considering conversational style can reveal another perspective on the "right time." In Chapter 4, I explained two styles that affect entering the conversation —high-involvement and high-considerateness. High-involvement speakers have particular ways of establishing rapport, and one of these is overlapping other speakers or finishing their sentences. Unlike interruption, which changes the topic of the conversation, overlapping indicates both speakers are on common ground. Speakers with a High-Considerateness Style allow about half a second between pauses. Speakers with this style may feel that overlapping is a problem if it happens often. If we have different turn-taking conventions than other speakers, we can feel that the flow of conversation has been thrown off. The conversation may feel jerky and we are suddenly aware of the other person's style of speaking. Even worse, we may attribute personality flaws to them.

In seminar several years ago, I proposed that students first take turns in a round robin fashion, giving a brief explanation of their thoughts about a journal article. The conversation would then follow, based on these ideas. Each person did take a turn, but instead of just listening to each person speak, one student commented about each speaker's point, and after six students had taken a turn, many other students began commenting as well rather than only listening. The students still gave the floor to each person around the room, but it took nearly the full two hours of our class time to hear from each student. When the round robin ended, some of the students commented on process. Jeffrey said, "It was my understanding we would go around the room and obviously that idea was thrown out the window." Immediately after his comment Linda comments in (12):

(12)
Well I think I was the one who threw it [the round robin] out the window and I'll tell you why . . . I think it started when Robin was talking and . . . I felt that everyone was kinda nervous about talking— she said something that kinda related to my thought . . . I think I was the first one who jumped into the pool and opened my mouth when it wasn't my turn. I thought it was adding support to the conversation.

Jeffrey was the third student to speak in the round robin, and he had not been one of the many contributors. Linda clearly was the student who talked the most, and her immediate reaction indicated that she had lost face: she explained that she wanted to support other speakers. As a high-involvement speaker, she felt that it was important to talk a lot to show that support. As the facilitator, I allowed the structure to change because so many excellent points were raised, but Jeffrey clearly would have preferred that everyone stick to the round robin plan. He felt that the rules for getting the floor were not followed. This incident raises issues about saving face as well as conversational style, and that will be explored in Chapter 7. From my point of view, I learned that if I announce a structure for seminar, it is best to follow it. This permits students to understand when and how much to talk, and since students are facing their own fears about interacting in seminar, this structure matters a great deal.

Conversation is an improvisation by speakers and hearers. We respond in real time to what others say or imply, and to our own perceptions of what they said or implied. We cannot always be conscious of what we are doing with our language or conversational turns. To refer back to the example in my seminar in (12), Linda became aware of her conversational style and its effects on the group only after Jeffrey pointed out the problem he had with the conversation. It is possible to imagine that students with High-Involvement Style are naturally dominant, or only concerned with their own ideas, or that they have a character flaw. Understanding different conversational styles— and the right time for expressing ideas in that style—helps us realize why seminars might not always have the structure we prefer and why some speakers seem to have the power to speak and others don't. At the same time we can begin to realize that our own approach to ideas and conversations is part of our social identity. Our social identities are always in process, so it is also important to remember that at certain moments in a conversation, we may draw on one identity more than another.

## CONCLUSION

Getting the floor is not just getting a turn at talk; it is having the power to initiate a topic that others join in examining. Students can have problems getting the floor because of their metaphorical understanding of seminar as well as their under-standing of collaborative learning. Gaining the agency to speak and get the floor comes with practice in developing a voice, having good ideas to contribute, and understanding our own metaphors for seminar. Simply categorizing students as talkative or quiet fixes that student in a particular category. Analyzing metaphors we use to describe seminars, on the other hand, allows us to teach more effectively.

## BEST PRACTICES

■ Bringing fruitful questions to seminar is one useful way to get the floor and students need to learn what a fruitful question is so they will have the confidence to raise it. Ask your students to bring a question to seminar and use the worksheet below to evaluate their questions. Doing this exercise in small groups for about 10 minutes will help students critically examine their questions. As you can see, the worksheet moves from a personal reaction to a deeper understanding of the text through analysis to a synthesis of what they have been learning. It also asks students to consider the phrasing of their question.

■ Help students realize that throwing out ideas in seminar is not enough. Ideas will have more value and interest to others if they are connected in some way to what others have said. For most students, taking notes of main points the group has covered is very useful in this process. You can provide a list of useful connecting statements:

— *As Sylvia was saying, On the same topic, To add to what you were saying,* or *On page 73 the author supports that idea;*

— *Your comment reminds me of what we were discussing earlier, Going back to an earlier point,* or *We could connect this idea to what Hiromi said earlier;*

## WORKSHEET ON EVALUATING SEMINAR QUESTIONS

Test each student's question in your group by addressing each bullet point below. The goal is to expand or clarify the question so that it opens a good conversation.

- Does the question come from a personal belief or opinion or experience? Does it expand or deepen or test that personal stance? If not, how can you change it so that it does one of those things?

- Does the question ask for an analysis of an argument, assumptions, themes, writing style, or methodology? If so, make sure that the question is worded to delve into the problems or issues you see.

- Does the question suggest a connection between ideas, theories, or concepts they have been learning in your class? Is it precise enough so that in your small group you can point to a connection?

- Does the question refer to specific pages in the text so that everyone has the same reference point? Does it provide enough background so that everyone understands the question?

- Is the question open-ended or does it suggest that there is one right answer? If it assumes one right answer, how can you reword the question so that it promotes collaborative learning and a good conversation?

— *I sort of agree but, It seems we are saying, I'm not sure that's the problem the author was trying to solve,* or *I disagree if you're arguing that.*

■ With your students, generate phrases students can use after they have stated their idea. Point out that hedges such as *Does that make sense? You know, I don't know* or *I'm not sure that's useful* can distract other students from the point being made. These hedges weaken the point and require that someone else make an assurance that the comment is helpful in order to save the speaker's face. Discuss other ways that students can conclude such as *This may not be the only way to look at the problem, I'm still working on this idea* or *Did anyone else have this idea?* These phrases invite others to respond on the same topic.

■ Students can sometimes become discouraged because others do not comment on their idea or attempt to answer their question. Although they voiced their idea, they did not really gain the floor. One reason for this is because they did not frame their comment in some way. I ask students to point to a specific page in the text where they have a comment or question and then wait a moment so that everyone can find the passage. If they want to reference earlier points in seminar, they need to briefly summarize those ideas. It is also helpful for them to state their point or ask their question in at least two ways. They can use phrases such as *in other words,* or *another way of asking this.* Taking up more time to contextualize their contribution helps everyone shift from what they were thinking about to this new point. Other students may be reflecting on the last points being made, their own question, or their daydreams. It is not a simple matter to listen carefully for extended periods of time, so students need to learn to frame their contributions to invite others to comment. Framing is a persuasive technique because it gives more explanation and therefore more weight and precision to the ideas being proposed.

- If you have only a few dominant or energetic speakers, and others are quiet, you can call for a pause and ask for a summary. I usually ask a quiet student to summarize, encouraging everyone to listen and to add more information. This activity can stimulate the group to reflect on how best to use the remaining time. Summarizing is a very important skill to learn, and providing a summary indicates to the group that active listening is fundamental to the conversation. Talkative students gain respect for students who listen carefully, as well.

- Students may also have difficulty gaining the floor if ideas are only lightly considered and generating ideas becomes more important than carefully considering them. If this seems to be a pattern, you might introduce a technique to slow down the conversation. One way is to introduce a talking stick, which originated as an indigenous practice. In order to speak, students and the faculty member need to indicate that they want the stick, and wait until they hold it before speaking. While holding the stick, the speaker has everyone's attention. Some faculty members use a ball of string instead. With this method, each speaker holds onto the string, tossing the ball to the next speaker. A visual web of the conversation develops. In both practices, passing an object slows down the conversation and helps students reflect longer on each speaker's words. I do have one caution about the ball of string. I videotaped one seminar using it (on the suggestion of the student facilitators), and one student told me in the video playback session that she saw the web of string as emphasizing those who were outside the circle, and she was disturbed by that. Another idea is to give each student three pennies. They spend a penny for each comment and they cannot speak if they have no more pennies, nor can they borrow someone else's. Because it takes more time to get the floor using these devices, students usually create more coherence in the conversation by referring to previous ideas and taking the time to elaborate on their points.

- Another structure that can help students learn to listen to each other and develop ideas more fully is using the fishbowl seminar. In this structure, students form two concentric circles. If your class is large, you may need to have several of these seating arrangements. Ten to twelve students sit in chairs in the small circle facing each other. Ten to twelve other students sit in a circle behind them. The job for the inner circle of students is to have a conversation on the text, usually with a specific assignment of analyzing a few chapters or sections of a text. The job for the outer circle is to listen and take notes only. After a designated period of time, such as 15 minutes, the students switch seats. The students in the inner circle incorporate or reflect on the ideas they heard as they complete their own assignment. Finally, the group gathers into one group and they continue the conversation by referring to what their classmates said earlier and building on that.

■ If you are part of a team that teaches sections of a large class, or part of a team teaching an interdisciplinary class, schedule your seminars at different times. You can then observe each other's seminars at least once each term. You can learn good practices by observing someone else's seminar and hearing the feedback from your colleagues about your practices is invaluable. If this is not possible, consider videotaping your seminar. You can then show all or part of it to your students. I have found that it is very revealing to watch your own seminar from a different perspective—that of the camera's lens. If you tell your colleagues and/or your students that your goal is understanding how speakers get the floor, everyone will have useful suggestions and observations.

■ Jack Mino (2013) was interested in integrative learning and used a "think aloud technique" to identify approaches students used. He interviewed students about their essays, asking them to read their papers aloud and explain where and how they integrated ideas from different disciplines. This would be a useful exercise if your students watched a videotape of your seminar. To analyze the interviews, he documented voice in writing and conversation by drawing on two methods from cognitive psychology, concept mapping and verbal protocol analysis, where students "think aloud" while performing a task. You can ask students to be explicit about the ways they see the course materials fitting together in seminar. Students could make cognitive maps in small groups and then compare their work. My faculty team created an exercise like this recently, and we had students create their maps on large sheets of paper. Then, in a poster session, one member of the team explained their poster for about three minutes, trading off with others in their team so that they could each view other posters. Many shy students like this sort of activity where they have a specific role. You can ask students to bring these sorts of integrative ideas into seminars in the future.

■ Having a better understanding of how they understand seminar metaphorically can help students feel more comfortable with the process. Here is a 15 minute exercise I use. I encourage you to take part in it with your students so that all seminar members have the same experience. Print a one-page double-sided worksheet. Tell your students to wait for your signal before turning the page over to see further instructions.

*[Page one]*

# YOUR INTERACTIONS IN SEMINAR

I. **Describe your interaction during seminars in writing (3–4 minutes):** You might ask yourself these questions: do you like to reflect for a while and formulate your point or do you talk as a way of thinking? Do you like to respond to provocative comments or are you more likely to let others respond? Do you get new ideas in seminar? Do you talk at length or in short bursts? Is it easy to get a turn to talk? Do you like to listen to other people? If you have facilitated seminars, what are your concerns in that role? Please use "I" for this exercise and use this page.

*[On the other side of the page, print the following:]*

II. **With a partner, look back over your writing and underline your metaphors (10 minutes).** Metaphors are figures of speech that create a comparison by representing one thing in terms of another. Often these are abstract concepts described as concrete objects. The following list may help you identify the metaphors you have used. After underlining your metaphors, note in the margins which of these categories are most appropriate. You may have metaphors that do not fit these categories, so consider creating another category for those.

- *Seminar is a Building*: Do you write about building on ideas, creating a foundation, working together, reinforcing ideas?
- *Seminar is a Stream*: Do you write about jumping into the conversation, letting the conversation flow, moving along too quickly or slowly?
- *Seminar is a Journey*: Do you want to arrive at a goal, watch for getting off track, take note of tangents, stay on a path?
- *Seminar is a Machine*: Do you want to be engaged or do you shift gears? Do you want seminar to run smoothly?
- *Seminar is a Container*: Do you notice ideas bubbling up, do ideas bounce around, are students in and out of the conversation?
- *Seminar is a Game*: Do you toss out ideas or toss them around the room, catch ideas? Do you describe other seminar members as doing a good job or not?
- *Seminar is a Community*: Do you write about how everybody is connected? Do you help others or describe others helping? Do you share ideas?

If there is time, you might ask for reflections on structures students might like to use given their new appreciation for their approach. Even if you cannot use all of these approaches due to time and/or your own comfort with them, everyone will have a new understanding of different conceptual systems at play.

# Chapter 6

# Performing Identities

In seminars, as we talk about our understanding of the text, we also construct, negotiate, and sometimes resist social identities. Social identity is not self-contained, unchanging, and definable; it is instead an on-going process that takes place in every conversation and seminar. Researchers use the term social identities as a way of distinguishing this on-going process from a fixed notion of the self. We are always negotiating multiple social identities as we talk and we draw on language to do that by choosing particular phrases, deciding whether to ask a question or make a statement, and using an informal or formal style, among other things.

Our identities come from our personal experiences and social interactions over time. These experiences are influenced by factors such as gender, race, ethnicity, social class, sexual orientation, age, abilities, education, religion, where we live, and where we come from. In addition, we do not construct our identities in isolation. Others have a hand in constructing our identities, too. One time at the grocery store, I was chatting with a colleague I had just encountered in the cleaning-items aisle. A man lingered nearby for a moment and then asked me how to clean stainless steel pans. I had not seen myself as an "expert in cleaning things," but he did, at least for that moment.

The male customer positioned me as "expert in cleaning things," and I understood his question to mean that because I am a woman in the cleaning aisle, I probably know how to clean things. In that instant my identity was no longer mine to define: it was created by another person's comment. Although I was actively shaping a different identity with my colleague, when I answered the man's question, I also validated my identity as an expert in cleaning things. Although we actively construct our identities in our interactions with others, negotiation is part of this process because the listener validates or rejects that identity.

Students in seminars are negotiating their identities as well as learning. One identity has to do with claiming or disclaiming authority as "someone who knows about this topic." Clearly, students may not always feel that they completely understand the text or have the authority to evaluate it so they are tentative in their comments. Or, they may remain silent because they do not have experience with academic discourse and the level of vocabulary and critical analysis overwhelms them. Usually all students feel confident in expressing opinions based on their own experiences, however. Gaining the authority to question a text or another student is part of what students learn in their community of practice in seminar.

## NEGOTIATING AUTHORITY

Authority is automatically conferred on faculty members in seminars because they have a clear status at their college or university and also because they will evaluate and grade the students. Even if this authority is symbolically reduced by arranging the seating in circles with no visual hierarchy, students cannot ignore this status. And yet, there is a measure of authority that is under negotiation in seminar. When a student asks a question, the faculty member may choose to wait for other students to respond, conferring authority on them by remaining silent. In some cases, it may be best for the faculty member to respond, and we need to make a judgment about those moments. If the question falls in my disciplinary expertise, and it seems worthwhile to provide information, I do so. On the other hand, in interdisciplinary courses, I have sometimes needed to mention my limited expertise about a topic when the question focused on a text chosen by a colleague in another discipline. Many faculty members adopt tactics to reduce their perceived authority in order to encourage conversation by teaching critical thinking, encouraging exploration, tolerating tangents, and nominating students to be facilitators.

The notion of who has authority in seminar is clearly based in part on students' beliefs about their own authority and the authority given to them by other students and the faculty member. It is through the moment-by-moment negotiations that are always present in seminars that we can see how authority and identity are intertwined. Rather than seeing authority as embodied in a person's status in seminar, we can see it as a product of the interaction between speakers. Sometimes this occurs very explicitly when we position ourselves as knowers; for example, we might say, *as a writer*, or *as a Southerner*, in order to introduce an idea in conversation. This phrase introduces the speaker as having the authority to talk about a particular topic. We can also position others by giving them a particular status, *Jon, you can probably speak to this since you've been in the same position*. We will look at this sort of explicit positioning in this chapter, but first we will turn to less noticeable ways that students position themselves as having authority through the stance that they take.

## STANCE

A speaker always has a particular stance about what they are saying, such as certainty, uncertainty, personal feelings, attitudes, value judgments, and assessments. Unlike English speakers, in Quechua a speaker must reveal this information. Quechua is a South American language spoken widely in Peru, Ecuador, and Bolivia, and there are three different grammatical markers that speakers must choose between to indicate what they know about the information they are giving: (1) the speaker has direct evidence for what they are saying and they are convinced that what they are saying is true; (2) the speaker is reporting something they have heard secondhand and making no claim about its truth; and (3) the speaker has inferred the evidence and is conjecturing, believing their statement to be true (Hintz, 2007). In English, of course, we can avoid stating the source of our evidence altogether. When students do that in seminar, they are often making a generalization or giving a personal opinion. More often, students give an indication of their evidence, and at the same time, they also reveal their relationship to other students by responding to what was just said, agreeing or disagreeing, or reinforcing the collaborative nature of the conversation.

Researchers studying large numbers of recorded conversations have found that the most ubiquitous stance markers that we all use are *I think* and *I don't know* (Baumgarten & House, 2010). *I think* signals to the listeners that the comment that follows is an assessment by the speaker. I have often heard experts interviewed in news stories use this clause, but it does not mean that it is only that expert's opinion; it can be a way of hedging. It allows the expert to rephrase in case of a challenge or if the facts change in some way. In seminars, it is very common for students to introduce their ideas with *I think*. They can also frame their comments and ideas in other ways so that others recognize their authority: they provide evidence for their idea, refer to a page in the text, link their idea to other texts in novel ways, and draw on their status as a collaborative learner.

When students provide evidence for their ideas, they usually take a particular stance that reveals how they know what they know. In a seminar on Kincaid's *It's a small place*, Stacey agrees with the previous speaker by using the phrase, "I felt the same that way that you did Liz." She agrees specifically with another student and also uses the same phrase Liz did, "I felt." This reveals her stance as one of personal emotion. Students used the first five minutes of their conversation to discuss the author's tone from a personal standpoint. Then a student asks, "Why did she write this book?" This question changes the focus from the students to the larger audience. After a couple of students respond, Elise gives her response in (1), using a number of hedges. Hedges soften or mitigate the force of statements and they can also make the speaker sound uncertain. Clauses such as *I think*, *I believe*, and *it is likely*, are common ways that students introduce an idea either because they are not sure about its plausibility or they want to test the waters with their idea. Other hedges like *maybe*, *sort of*, *kind of*, and *in a way* are also used for these purposes. In (1) I highlight hedges in bold type:

(1)

*Elise:*  Um as far as like who she wrote the book for↑ when I was reading it **I was also thinking that maybe** she wrote the book for the people that she left be*hind* when she went– came to the US that it was a book um written in part like **almost it seemed like almost** like an apology and **in a way** that she um that she *was*n't there ta– ta be like going through this

Elise's stance comes from her own experience as a reader: "when I was reading it I was also thinking." Her hedges indicate that this is only a possible explanation, as does her use of "like" in defining the author's purpose as an apology. Using several hedges invites collaboration from other students on this question and several other students follow by offering their own interpretations.

## BALANCING AUTHORITY AND SOLIDARITY

In another class, a student has a different question, "Why are we reading this book right now? It's a complete mystery to me." This question is an important one in a team-taught interdisciplinary course where the connections between texts, lectures, and assignments may not be clear to all students. The faculty member does not immediately answer the question, so Jodi takes the opportunity to do so. Jodi is making two points, but only the first is excerpted in (2):

(2)

| | | |
|---|---|---|
| 1 | *Jodi:* | I have two points from a while ago ((laughs)) |
| 2 | *Others:* | ((laughter)) |
| 3 | *Jodi:* | Um first↑ oh first things are your question ( ) throughout |
| 4 | | like why are we reading this book right now is this labor history |
| 5 | | Um I was gonna say that it has *so* much to do with it |
| 6 | | because be*fore*– this was forty years after slavery↑ |
| 7 | | but be*fore* the en*tire* like *country* depended on slavery |
| 8 | | like that was like the means of pro*duc*tion and money |
| 9 | | and *then* all of a sudden we don't have *sla*very anymore |
| 10 | | so where does labor go from *there* |
| 11 | | and it goes to *mills* |
| 12 | | it goes to a different form of slavery like mill owners and stuff |
| 13 | | like that so I just wanta throw that out |
| 14 | | that's how I think the book is important ((laughing)). |

In the first four lines Jodi paraphrases the question, "Why are we reading this book right now?" This positions her to answer it and alerts the group to her intention. They indicate their solidarity by laughing with her. She introduces her answer in line 5 with "I was gonna say." This phrase, together with her first statement, indicate she has been reflecting on what she will say. She then briefly explains the importance of economic change from slavery to factories (lines 6–12) using the analogy of slavery to describe this change for the workers. By using this analogy, she makes a powerful point. Both her introduction and her analogy create a stance of an engaged, knowledgeable student. Then in the last two lines the student reduces her authority to assert solidarity with the other students: "I just wanta throw that out." With this comment and her informal style, she positions herself as a group member who had a thought and threw it out. In addition, by framing her statement with laughter at the beginning and end, she also reduces her authority. So while she positions herself as having the answer to another student's question, she creates an opening for others to throw out their ideas at the end, because that's all she is doing. In this case, no one else follows with alternative explanations for the question of why they are reading this book. The reason could be that Jodi continued holding the floor and followed this point with another, unrelated one. Usually when there are two points in someone's turn, only the last one is taken up by the listeners.

Besides drawing on information in class, referring directly to the text gives students authority because they have clearly read the text carefully. In (3), Derek refers to the author, quotes from the text, and then presents his own deduction using hedges (in bold type). He is disagreeing with the previous speaker:

(3)

| | | |
|---|---|---|
| 1 | *Derek*: | She talks about that a lot when she's talking about colonialism |
| 2 | | And uh she talks on page 36 |
| 3 | | I wrote in– at my side notes that we keep seeing this type of thing |
| 4 | | where she says "and you leave" meaning the colonial people |
| 5 | | ((reads text)). And she also talks in another part of the book |
| 6 | | About being released from being in control by the colonial groups. |
| 7 | | But the colonial structure still exists. So **I guess** I can't look |
| 8 | | at it as they're not really governing themselves. If you had |
| 9 | | gone back three hundred years and then left them alone |
| 10 | | and now said well hey this is the way they wanna run their country |
| 11 | | then I **probably** would be more likely to say that well then |
| 12 | | that–that's fine. But **I don't think** that they're really in |
| 13 | | control of their own lives. **I think** all of the things left |
| 14 | | by colonialism are still there. |

**87**

Derek refers to his own thinking while reading the book as Jodi did in (2). In line 3 he says, "I wrote in– at my side notes." His evidence, then, is his own thinking and note-taking while reading. In lines 8–12 he provides his own explanation for why colonialism still affects the people using hedges *I guess, probably, I don't think, I think*. Note that if he had not used these phrases, his comment would have more authority. He provides a hypothetical conversation and interjects an imaginary conversation with a student he disagrees with. Then in lines 12–14 he presents a summary. He gains authority by presenting this persuasive argument. His use of hedges softens his disagreement and invites further discussion on the topic, a move towards solidarity. He also deepened the conversation by giving an example (the hypothetical conversation) to explain why he agrees with the author and disagrees with the previous student.

In (1)–(3) students used evidence from class materials, the text, and their own experience. In (4), Will makes a connection to another text in the class, getting murmurs of appreciation for his comment. This sort of synthesis is higher order thinking and everyone recognizes that even though he has trouble articulating his idea. When he finishes speaking, several students say, "that's a good point" and there is a general murmur of approval that does not occur in other parts of this seminar. In fact, that sort of larger group approval is rare.

(4)

*Will*:    And uh I think the first section↑ the way it was written↑ Kind of is– kind of looking– it's saying you– it's looking– It's kind of taking the maybe the first colonialists' view or maybe th– the stereotypes of (1) like the– a tourist will take and project onto uh the people (.) like the– of the country where they're touring and reversing the gaze and turning it around onto the tourists [. . .] and just returning the gaze basically [. . .]

Will hedges a great deal and often reformulates his ideas as he is speaking, but the notion of reversing the gaze is powerful, and it resonates with other students. They had learned about the notion of the gaze, but Will was the first to try to explain the way that it works through stereotyping in this text. His comments position him as knowledgeable on a major topic in the conversation.

One of my students, Kaitlin Maltz, clearly explains the function of hedges in seminar for an exercise in my class, Art of Conversation, in 2008:

The most common words I've observed in seminar are hedges. I find that individuals, aside perhaps from the professor, are quite hesitant to assert their opinions/observations without first prefacing their responses with *I think*, *I mean,* or *When I read this, I thought*. Although at first glance these hedges may appear to be used by students who are merely unsure of their response, I find that there is perhaps more going on than that. I believe such hedges function, at least partially, to define the community of seminar students. When one begins her contribution with a tentative hedge (and occasionally goes on to insert *you know* or *I'm not quite sure but*) she is identifying herself not as an expert on a particular subject or an authority figure, but declaring herself as 'equal' to the rest of the seminar group. I've found that students are continually vigilant against offending others in the group, a concern that often manifests in a smattering of *but I don't know* trailing off at the end of comments. This, of course, is partially due to the nature of seminars, where no participant is really the 'authority' on the text, not having written it. Hedging it seems, provides a more open, non-judgmental atmosphere and encourages (ideally) more individuals to speak; they effectively perpetuate the community of speakers.

Maltz observes that although hedges may reduce a speaker's authority indicating tentativeness, they also function to create a community. This is an insightful observation because our words and phrases rarely have just one meaning. In this case, hedges can create solidarity with other students and that is as important as the power of being an authority on the text for most students.

In all of these examples, we see students creating various stances that position them as knowledgeable or tentative authorities. In all but the first example, other students respond to these statements indicating they have merit either by saying so as in (4), or by responding directly to what that person has said. Gaining authority as a knowledgeable student in seminar has to do with framing the idea as well as providing evidence. By framing an idea I mean providing enough background that others can understand the point. As we have seen, this needs to be done while asserting solidarity with other students as a collaborative learner. Students do this primarily by hedging, so that they don't sound pedantic or overbearing. They can also use words such as *obviously*, *of course*, *it goes without saying* to state their authority as knowledgeable without hedging but this is less common.

In some cases, students reduce their authority because of reactions from others. Researchers examining collaborative learning among freshmen recorded a case when a student did not hedge her authority (Benwell & Stokoe, 2002, p. 447). In (5) students are discussing what they will write in a collaborative document:

(5)
1   *S1:*   does rehearsal (.) help (.) retain the stimulus
2        (1.0)
3   *S2:*   oohh! [hahahaha
4   *S3:*        [hahahaha
5   *S4:*        [hahahaha=

**89**

6   *S1:*   =haha (.) phew (.) [where did that come from? hahaha
7   *S2:*                      [haha have you swallowed the dictionary!

S1 suggests a phrase, "does rehearsal help retain the stimulus" in line one, and then claims not to be the source of those words in line 6 by asking, "Where did that come from?" The laughter from other students and the comment, "have you swallowed the dictionary!" indicate that she had taken on too much authority by using an academic phrase. Balancing authority with solidarity is important for students to gain the floor.

## LABELING OTHERS

Besides positioning themselves as a potential authority, students and faculty members grant authority explicitly by positioning other people. One way that is not useful is to label speakers with one social identity. This occurs when students or faculty members turn to a particular student and say, for example, "Peter, you're Native American, what do you think about this question?" In my research and in my own teaching, students have pointed out that they do not appreciate being singled out as speaking for an entire group. In my survey of students regarding seminar practices, for example, students were not asked to identify themselves with an ethnic group, but two volunteered that information. One was Hispanic, the other Hawaiian. Both felt strongly that they had been singled out in seminar as having a particular ethnicity yet neither wanted to be in the position of representing their ethnic group. Several other students in that study remarked that they had noticed students being singled out, and that this was undesirable.

Students I have spoken with who are given an ethnic or racial label in seminar cannot imagine how they can speak for the broad diversity of their ethnic group. To test this notion, select one of your social identities and ask yourself if you can speak for all members of that group. If you or someone else identifies a student as having a particular ethnicity, you may also be implying that no one else in the group has that ethnicity or has experience with that ethnicity. Yet, many students are mixed in terms of their ethnicity or they have family members with ethnicities different than their own, and their experience and deep understanding of social issues can be silenced if only one or a few people assumed to have a particular ethnicity are asked to speak. In addition, if the student identified chooses to speak after being singled out, their own point of view becomes subsumed into the "Hispanic" or "African-American" point of view. Their own individuality and voice become lost. Note also that "white" is not usually considered an ethnic group, and in seminars I recorded I did not find anyone saying, "You're white, what do you think about this?"

This point about labeling highlights the ways that dominant groups—in this case white students and faculty members—create the "other" from targeted groups. Patricia Hill Collins (1993), a well-known sociologist, writes that she heard many African-American students over the years complain that their professors never called on them except when an issue relating to their race came up. For the faculty member, the urge to hear testimonials about lived experience to illustrate a concept may be well intentioned, but Collins points out that this sort of performance on cue amounts to voyeurism by privileged people. The privileged in this case are those who are members of the dominant class of white, and in this case, well-educated people. Collins sees voyeurism as a common pattern in the ways privileged people see the lives of people of color and the poor as interesting for their entertainment value.

Students may also feel labeled not because of an explicit comment but because of the nonverbal behavior of other members of the students. Buttny (1997, p. 494) asked small groups of students to talk about a video, "Racism 101," outside of class and record their conversation. In (6) he presents a transcription of two African-American students (I have simplified the transcription a little):

(6)
*F:*   So you never feel individualistic, you also feel as if you're M the black guy in class=

*M:*   =Yeah exactly

*F:*   So everything you do is because you're black

*M:*   Every time something regarding race comes up they go like whoosh and I'm in the corner going like my God why you looking at me I'm not the only– I didn't like die and say I wanted to be a spokesman for my race somewhere ya know if there was an application I didn't put it in ya know. But they look at you like that and unfortunately there's very little I can do about that, because I am the only Black in almost all of my classes I'm the only Black person in there.

The male speaker makes a humorous comment, "they go like whoosh," referring to the collective turning of heads to look at him that makes a sound and moves the air. He then uses reported speech, introducing what is going through his mind with "going like." His conclusion is, "unfortunately there's very little I can do about that, because I am the only Black in almost all of my classes I'm the only Black person in there." M feels that students are waiting for his comments and labeling him as someone who would have insight, but because his social identities are reduced to his race alone, he feels he cannot respond with his own point of view.

Besides race or ethnicity, a student's gender can be highlighted. In a conversation about sweat-shops in developing countries where women were the workers, Mitt makes a comment and Tricia responds by labeling him a white male in (7). Nancy moves the conversation towards ideas rather than labels.

(7)

*Mitt*: I have a hard time you know really uh you know feeling bad for– for a lot of these situations when you know I mean we've all had ba– crappy jobs where it's just like you know I've been at work for 12 hours with not a half hour break but no break and stuff like that and I– the point being that uh- it's going on everywhere=

*Trish*: =You're speaking from a white male– you– no matter how sympathetic you are to women you're still in a world that's a white male hier– hierarchy and you still no matter how sympathetic you are still a white male

*Mitt*: Right. But

*Trish*: =Situation. You– you have the advantage sitting right in your chair right now

*Mitt*: I– I do. You think so ((sarcastically)).

*Trish*: Yes

*Mitt*: You think I'm I have– I'm exclusive from being uh– excluded from being exploited at all?

*Trish*: No. You're part of your system but you also have the advantage of that system.

*Mitt*: Hmm.

*Nancy*: You know from what you just said? I see a lot of differences in– in the book and what those women are going through or what we saw this morning and I'm just ( )

*Mitt*: Right ( ) But the point being that you know that there's an exploitatation going on everywhere. And it's– and you know I mean that's– that's the nature of work really. That's the nature of labor. That– that you know people are being used for the– for so many hours a day and– and you know so it's the capitalist way but ( )

*Trish*: I don't think men and women are being used exactly in the same way though.

*Mitt*: Fair enough. ((shrugs))

Trish labels Mitt as a white male with an advantage because he is living in a white male hierarchy. She reinforces the fact that she is different from him by saying, "you're part of your system but you also have the advantage of your system." Nancy points out that they are not talking about one person's personal experience with work, but the materials they are discussing: "I see a lot of differences in– in the book and what those women are going through and what we saw this morning." (They had seen a documentary film.) Her contribution shifts the perspective for both of the other speakers. Mitt's evidence moves to the capitalist system, "there's exploitation going on there," and Trish in her last line refers to men and women, not Mitt. This shift in perspective reduces the focus on labeling.

Although Mitt is labeled as a white male and he agrees by saying, "Right," he also resists this labeling by asking, "You think I– I'm . . . excluded from being exploited at all?" This conversation shows the negotiation of identity that can happen when we are positioned by others. Mitt indirectly includes himself and Trish as workers in the capitalist system, repositioning himself at the end of this transcription.

A different student, who participated in that same seminar and watched the edited version with me about a week later, told me he considered this seminar to be a "feminar," blending "seminar" with "feminist" to coin this term. He told me he had to be convinced by a friend not to leave during a break. I was surprised by this comment because he had been an active member of seminar in other moments and there was no observable indication that he was uncomfortable in his words or nonverbal actions. Because he was a white male, he may have felt accused of being privileged even though Trish did not include him in her overt labeling. His resistance to that positioning was evident in his description of the conversation as a feminar.

There are also times in seminar when everyone feels labeled. The following example (8) is from a student who was tape recorded in my student survey:

(8)
There was a Hawaiian girl in my seminar. We were talking about exploration of the Americas by the Europeans. She felt the implication from the conquest of the Hawaiian Islands by Cook and his expedition and all the later explorers. It made all us white people feel really guilty. She was the only non-white person. She felt bad, too. She felt very victimized. She felt it affected her cultural identity today, too, even though we all really respected her. We carried on these roles somehow through history that had been portrayed in the explorers we were studying. That was a very vivid experience.

In (6) and (7), students applied labels to other students or to themselves, but it is also clear that resistance to the labels can occur and that this resistance may or may not occur in the conversation.

## LABELING ONESELF

In a different class, I present a student's comments as she questions her own identity and labels herself. Students were discussing whether or not they agreed with the author's argument that the image of Aunt Jemima on boxes of pancake mix is a racist one of a nanny and a slave. Two voice objections early on. Dan says, "I just really take issue with the whole idea that we white Americans are responsible for perpetrating this racist symbol because it's still on the shelf." After some discussion, Haley asks, "If you hadn't read this book would anyone see this as a racist symbol?" A couple of students quickly respond that they have always seen the image as a racist symbol. Jenny then begins to think aloud about her own position as a consumer, and holds the floor for just over two minutes. By "holding the floor" I mean that although others speak, the topic remains the one she introduced, and she responds to other students' comments. Early in her two minutes of holding the floor she comments in (9):

(9)

*Jenny*:  On page 175 it said racism is so engrained in some peoples' psyche that they don't *know* what's offensive. And I was like, is that me? But I don't believe so.

*FM*:  [That's a great question for all of us ((quietly))

Jenny uses reported speech, quoting herself asking "is that me?" while she was reading. This is a way of distancing herself from the author's claim that racism is engrained in some people's psyche. She may or may not be accurately reporting what she actually said or thought at the time she was reading page 175, but reporting on this thought allows her to evaluate it not only for herself but for the group: "I don't believe so." This is a stance that gives her authority as a knowledgeable student because she has clearly been reflecting on the images of Aunt Jemima prior to seminar.

As others briefly comment on her points, she refers to the author's argument: "nannies symbolize motherhood, service, love, and *slavery*. Now the thing I overlook is the slavery." She is thinking as she talks, trying to resolve the rhetorical question she had posed just moments ago in the quote, "Is that me?" The conversation turns to whether or not the Aunt Jemima image is or could be offensive to African-Americans. (No students indicate they are African-American.) A few moments later, she asks, "So am I a racist? That's a big question."

Jenny's question has several functions: first, she questions her own social identity; second, she demonstrates her learning in her struggle with considering the author's argument; third, she invites a yes/no response in the form of her question. By tentatively applying a label to herself that is highly offensive to herself and the other students, she is testing another identity, realizing that it is not fixed and that she may not understand it completely. Her stance as an active, reflective thinker willing to challenge her identities helps engage others to consider the author's thesis rather than rejecting it.

This may be why Leila, who is sitting next to Jenny, speaks next. She identifies herself as a minority, and answers Jenny's question: "No, you are not a racist." Then she gives an explanation excerpted in (10):

(10)

*Leila*:  I think a lot of people just don't realize how much power they have. Like I mean I'm a minority in a predominantly white school and

[. . .] they're like well they're my friend ((puts her hand on Jenny's shoulder)) you know their first comment to me is oh well I have black friends or I have Hispanic friends or something like that but I think that people just aren't aware of the power they have [. . .] even you know they– you have it.

Leila shifts pronouns in the last line. She is really not talking about "they" but about "you." After this statement, several other students make comments, and then Leila explains how to tell if something's offensive: "Just flip it . . . If you don't do it in one ethnic group, why do it to others?" Leila's stance as a minority student allows her to assess Jenny's question and point out that Jenny and others have power and privilege that they do not acknowledge.

It is clear in this conversation that the students are comfortable with each other and they share a goal of critically analyzing the text. They listen to each other and test their understanding of the author's thesis. Jenny positions herself as a mother and a possible racist. The conversation made her learning possible. Dan takes issue with the idea that he is somehow complicit with the selling of the pancake mix, positioning himself and others as "we white Americans." Haley questions whether anyone would recognize the image as a slave, positioning herself as a member of the dominant white society. Instead of rejecting or questioning the author's thesis, Jenny plays what Peter Elbow (1986) calls "the believing game." She considers the idea that she doesn't know what is offensive and although she holds that idea at arm's length (through her gesture in the example above), she deepens the conversation by considering it carefully rather than critiquing it. Elbow points out that "the doubting game," the practice of rejecting an argument, is a primary way of learning in academia, and that by practicing "the believing game" we can develop the perspectives on a problem to a greater extent.

In another seminar, computer-programming students have moved off topic to problems Microsoft was having with software piracy in some markets around the world. One student introduces the topic of the Asian market and copyright issues. The faculty member begins to ask for an elaboration when she is interrupted by a student from China, Han, who announces, "I am Asian." The transcript in (11) focuses on his comment only:

(11)

| | |
|---|---|
| *Han*: | I'm Asian. I know a lot of piracy over there so |
| | ((laughter)) |
| *Han*: | That's true. |
| *FM*: | So do you so do you |
| *Han*: | [We admit that. Yeah it's a lot of piracy because– because |
| *Han*: | Goldman then you know they take money from here and there ( ) |

*Matt*:  Yeah it's– it's not just software

*Han*:  [It's a big business. People re-re-reproduce software from Microsoft

*Han*:  they sell that one. They sell like one third of the price of the original or less that that (.) So Microsoft really really not trustworthy of Asian market.

Han first announces he is Asian, affirms there is a lot of piracy in Asia, and then says, "We admit that" in line 3. His identity expands from the personal ("I") to a social identity of Asian government officials and/or business people with his use of "we." He next explains how the piracy occurs, which further underscores his knowledge of this issue. By positioning himself as Asian, he immediately gains the floor and gives more information than previous students had provided about the problem of software piracy, establishing his authority on the topic.

The next example comes from one of my seminars. Students are discussing an article about gender and language. In (12) Sean refers to his experience with the term *sissy*:

(12)

*Sean*:  Some boys are considered sissies because they can't play the game. That according to this article is the reason– I know that's why I was considered a sissy and I'm not considered a sissy these days. I'm considered a homosexual. Next?

The authors of the text had mentioned that more research should be done on tomboys, but they did not mention that research should be done on sissies. Sean stated that his ideas about "sissy" are not yet clear, but here he draws a parallel between being a sissy as a child and a homosexual as an adult. There is laughter, and the student next to him begins her turn, focusing on her own ideas. It was possible to comment on Sean's point, and some students had commented on other contributions, but in this case no one did. This could have happened because he abruptly ended his turn, and called for the next speaker. Sean's positioning as homosexual gives weight to his thinking about future research that needs to be done, and it was useful in a conversation about language and gender to point out how adults position children. It was also risky to identify himself as gay. Depending on seminar topics, this risk can pay off in terms of positioning oneself as knowledgeable about a particular issue or question.

## CONCLUSION

In recent years, I have noticed that students volunteer more information about their social identities than previously. This could be due to the prevalence of social media in our lives where self-revelation is commonplace, and it can also be due to growing social acceptance of a variety of lifestyles. As students and faculty position themselves and others, they are shaping the conversation, and they are also shaping social identities. As we have seen, being restricted to a particular social identity can stop some students from entering the conversation.

The practices that we have examined are not limited to seminars, and can occur in other communities of practice. In seminars students balance their authority as knowledgeable students with their desire to show solidarity with other students. They actively shape their social identities as learners. As students become more familiar with seminar and the other students, they become more comfortable using academic discourse. Their development depends in large part on our facilitation of the conversation.

## BEST PRACTICES

- Consider your authority in seminar and how you position yourself as the instructor. Consider your implicit social positioning as well and ask yourself if there are blind spots you might address as you're reading the texts or facilitating seminars. Have you chosen texts that are all written by white men, for example? What are your criteria for selecting texts?

- Besides trying to express their ideas, students need to learn to position themselves as knowledgeable in an academic context. You can address the ways that students introduce their ideas and help them see that their opinions should be based on close reading of the text. Ask that they always bring the text in hard copy or on an electronic device; ask that they refer to specific page numbers in their comments; and make sure they wait to give everyone time to find the passage they are referring to. Model how to do this. Students may need instruction on how to read a novel, how to find an argument, and how to read a journal article.

- Ask students to consider the assumptions and stance of the authors they are reading. When do the authors use hedges? Do they present ideas and arguments as facts? Do they assume that their ideas apply to all people regardless of their social identities? Discuss the impossibility of being completely objective.

- Watch for the ways you and your students position group members. It is very effective to point out that a student had earlier made a comment that is relevant, or otherwise position students as knowledgeable according to their comments, but choosing to comment on one of their social identities reduces their agency in the conversation.

- Discuss how students can position themselves as knowledgeable in seminar. Some students may be unfamiliar with academic discourse or not feel as smart as other

**97**

students. I provided a list of ways academics approach a text in Chapter 1, Best Practices. Consider focusing on just one way for two weeks to help your students practice. If they are new to seminar, allow students to refer to their own experience occasionally. Gaining a voice begins with offering a comment. The next step is learning critical thinking practices and shaping comments to be persuasive.

■ Consider having students act as facilitators. If you have a large class, you can divide your students into groups for half of the time, each with a student facilitator. This works well if all students are required to post a question on the class website at least an hour before seminar. Facilitators can meet to read them and find themes that their groups can discuss. When the whole class comes together, these groups can report on their conversations. Learning to facilitate helps students listen carefully to what is going on in the conversation in order to guide it. It also gives them clear authority for a short time. This is particularly useful to quiet students.

# Chapter 7

# Agreeing to Disagree

Seminars are designed for collaborative learning but collaborative learning does not mean students will only have cooperative conversations that end in consensus, nor does it mean that all discussions should end by agreeing to disagree. What is essential in seminar is agreeing that disagreements will occur and that there are many ways to express disagreement that will stimulate new ideas and more learning. Learning is a lot of work, and students need to test their own ideas, and react to those of others, challenging or critiquing those ideas.

Part of the work involves creating an argument to support or reject ideas. The words we use to describe what's going on in arguments such as, *they shot down her idea*, *he took their side*, *she fortified her position*, and *you used the usual strategies to win*, all point to an underlying metaphor—ARGUMENT IS WAR. Besides winning or losing an argument, we have opponents, we gain or lose ground, and we defend ourselves. George Lakoff and Mark Johnson (1980), who revealed this metaphorical way of speaking about argument, pointed out that we have no other way of talking about what's going on in an argument because this is how we think about it. It is a verbal battlefield.

## ARGUING TO WIN AND ARGUING TO PERSUADE

We use the word *argument* in two ways that have many similarities. One type, arguing to win, is found in everyday conversation. It is often heated, and winning is the reason to engage in the argument in the first place. It usually has two sides and the point is to defend a position. Speakers stay with their position even if it seems untenable. Using sarcastic or derisive tones, speaking quickly, loudly, and angrily are all possible features. The second type, arguing to persuade, is used in seminars and other academic discourses, especially essays and research papers, to mean presenting a claim supported by strong evidence from reputable sources. There are usually multiple perspectives about this claim and it is important to acknowledge them and show why, given these other views, the author's claim is better. Revealing assumptions about a perspective and evaluating the source of evidence is often a focus in academic discourse. Arguing to persuade, like arguing to win can be heated, two-sided, and people can stick to untenable positions but the academic argument should draw on previous research and not just personal experience.

Students need to learn to distinguish between these two types of argument as part of their learning in seminars. Some students are socialized to engage in arguments to win as a regular form of disagreement and they are unfamiliar with the form and function of academic argument. In addition, in the larger context of the media, some political discourse on talk radio, public blogs, and cable television news analysis programs can be characterized as arguing to win, or, as Sobieraj and Berry (2011) call it, arguing with "outrage talk." This is verbal competition using exaggeration, mockery, insults, and name calling that is clearly uncivil. These forums for public discourse have expanded enormously in the last five years and their audience is growing. The entertainment value of these sites can influence students, and they may borrow some of these techniques because they are so pervasive. Arguing to win can create a hostile atmosphere for students who expect an argument to persuade. And, depending on the topic and who is speaking, students can feel attacked if someone harshly critiques their ideas. If no one else comes into the conversation to defend their idea, they can feel exposed and powerless.

Given this potential for war, the ways that students disagree can profoundly influence the direction of the conversation. We probably all have had a moment, for example, when we hear another person make a statement that we know for a fact to be wrong. We have a choice of saying, *you're wrong* or *that's just not true*. Depending on the situation, our response could cause the other person to get angry or begin an argument to win. Instead, we could use other expressions that soften our disagreement depending on the status of the other person, the situation, our own investment in the conversation, and who is listening. For example, we could say, *are you sure about that?* This gives the speaker time to retract the statement but it is also a challenge. We could also change the topic to avoid confrontation. In these possible responses, the underlying concern is to show respect for the other person. A different way to respond is to agree partially: *you make a good point but.* By agreeing partially, we indicate that we share some common ground.

## WHY FACEWORK MATTERS

Why does this matter? A well-known sociologist, Erving Goffman (1967), illustrated that in every conversation we are oriented towards maintaining our face, which is a positive image of ourselves that includes self-respect and a level of confidence. As we maintain our face, we need to take note of what others say or think because we are not the sole agents constructing our selves—others in the conversation are involved as well. We want to maintain a positive image of our selves so we are always working to maintain it. One way of doing that is to save face for others and show consideration for their feelings because this reflects positively on us. Goffman claimed that in conversation we are not primarily concerned with information sharing as much as the ritual of maintaining face, which he calls facework. Facework is a mutual acceptance in each interaction that each person wants to maintain face and that considerateness for others needs to be taken into account. Face also has to do with showing others that you like them and that you share their concerns and interests.

Facework does not always lead to a balanced or harmonious conversation. If we feel that others respect our face, we can fish for compliments or challenge someone to see if we can get away with it. Sometimes we feel we need to "get through" a meeting, so we may interact very minimally and others may feel a lack of respect. Sometimes we can't or won't get hints from others that we're acting inappropriately. We usually notice when we're being impolite, which is also a rupture in the ritual work of facework. In these situations, we threaten another speaker's face. Sometimes we don't know we're threatening someone else's face, of course. This can happen in cross-cultural situations or when we're not paying attention to the cues around us or when we don't know enough about the people we're talking to. Nonetheless, we are generally expected to show respect or common ground to maintain everyone's face. Goffman's notion of facework helps explain why we might laugh at someone's joke or witticism even if we don't think it is funny: we're showing common ground by agreeing on what is funny. It also explains why someone might apologize if they've just monopolized a conversation with a detailed complaint. In that case, they have risked imposing on the listener. Sometimes not saying anything at certain points in a conversation can threaten the other person's face because they can perceive silence as not showing respect or common ground.

We may not think consciously about these choices of response, but each of us has a large repertoire of linguistic strategies that we learned through our cultural socialization. Because our choices are sometimes unconscious, we can say something with unintended results and threaten the other person's face. And, there are times when we are not concerned with saving someone else's face. We might be engaged in a political debate or need to yell at someone out of frustration. In the heat of the moment we might give a sharp retort rather than softening it. Also, some relationships allow for ignoring a complaint, challenging it, or teasing. But these relationships can still be ruptured if someone goes too far. The rupture can be repaired in the conversation or at another time, but Goffman cautions that repair could cause other difficulties. In this case repair means apologizing for something we said. Apologies can be difficult to accomplish because we may not meet the wronged person's expectations. We might not choose the best words or apologize for all aspects of the situation. If we wait too long to apologize, our attempt at repair can also cause further problems.

Importantly, our face does not remain the same all of the time. It is a positive image of ourselves, and our different identities, relationships, and goals in the conversation can change the ways in which we present ourselves. In seminars, for example, I consider my role as facilitator to be more important than my role as teacher or evaluator. I work actively to encourage students to elaborate on their ideas, to respond to each other, and to delve into the text. If a student misquotes what I said in a lecture or makes a statement that is illogical in the context of our class, I try not to jump in immediately to correct the student. As a facilitator, I wait for other students to do this work. This lessens the impact of the correction and indicates to the students that they are responsible for the content of the conversation.

In conversations, then, we are always negotiating face and our social relationships moment by moment and, as we have seen in Chapters 4 and 6, we are also negotiating identity and solidarity as we time ourselves in an intricate improvisation. Face can be part of a larger, more permanent notion of status and respect in society, which is very important in Chinese culture, for example. Here, though, we are concerned with the moment by moment negotiations in conversations. In seminars, the interaction of facework, identity, solidarity, and timing can cause students to lose face indirectly. In a seminar I discussed in Chapter 5, for example, the plan I announced was to hold a 15 minute round robin, and in part because of one student with a High-Involvement Style, it lasted nearly the entire two hours. In the last few minutes, a student pointed out the rules of the round robin as one reason he did not contribute more. His comment caused the high-involvement speaker to lose face, which she indicated by immediately justifying her many comments as trying to be helpful. She tried to reposition herself from talker to facilitator of talk in her apology. Even though there was no face threat directed specifically at her, her response indicated that her face was threatened.

Face threats can be avoided by agreeing and by softening disagreements. Agreeing generally indicates common ground and solidarity because it indicates that the speakers are thinking in the same way. Agreeing can give face to the other person and it is part of what we can call supportive facework (Watts, 2003). No expression of solidarity or lack of solidarity will last throughout a seminar or all seminars in a class, however. Solidarity can be ruptured by disagreement, because disagreeing threatens the face of the person who is being disagreed with. Students have many ways of softening their disagreements to avoid a rupture by using supportive facework. How students disagree reveals the level of a possible face threat as well as the solidarity or lack of solidarity they want to express. In arguments to win, they may be more concerned with power and authority than with saving face. In a debate, students are concerned with scoring points rather than attending to the opponent's face. In an attempt to sound authoritative, a student may dismiss someone else's idea in order to gain the floor and announce their own idea. Establishing the goal of seminar as collaborative learning and not arguing to win or debating, helps students be more aware of the words they use to disagree. Explicit ways of expressing agreement and disagreement, *I agree* or *I disagree*, are not common in my data in face-to-face seminars; instead, students express their ideas using a wide array of approaches. Understanding the range of practices that students use to disagree, from neutral to supportive facework to face threatening can help facilitators recognize what is going on and whether or not to step in. Supportive facework is most useful in developing persuasive arguments and allowing students to develop new ideas and perspectives.

## DISAGREEING IN A NEUTRAL WAY

In cases where students present ideas with no explicit agreement or disagreement implied, they are most often answering a question or brainstorming and they each present different points of view in a rapid and rather short sequence. The metaphor of tossing out ideas describes this situation. This is a neutral activity in terms of facework. Students allow ideas to be presented with no assessment or judgment—even if the ideas are quite different—because they have joined together in trying to answer a question. Quite often students preface their comment with *I think*, but there may be no preface at all. In (1) students generate some ideas that answer the faculty member's (FM) question about the protagonist in Horatio Alger's *Raggedy Dick* and then a student changes the focus of the conversation. I only present the beginnings of each student's comments to focus on the way that it is introduced.

(1)
FM: Well it's interesting that you said that– that working for somebody *else* is part of being respectable. Why?
Zillah: Somebody would then value him [. . .]
Ava: Um Raggedy didn't have parents so I think in a way [. . .] there was an underlying need for a father figure [. . .]
Craig: I think also he wanted the stability of belonging [. . .]
Nolan: Another thing I noticed is that he went from now– the necessities– the moment to looking at the big picture looking down the road. A week from now. A month from now. A year from now [. . .]

In (1), the faculty member poses a question about the relationship between being respectable and working for someone else and four students respond in turn. Zillah begins by saying, "somebody would then value him." This appears to provide a theme for the next two speakers. She is followed by Ava, who specifies the need for a father figure and Craig who focuses on belonging to a family or group. Nolan, however, changes the topic by saying, "Another thing I noticed." He does not link his comment explicitly to the question, but he deepens the conversation with another perspective on working for someone else. The first three responses, then, can be seen as building upon each other, and Nolan moves the topic. The students provide four perspectives with no judgment or reference to each other's comments. This is a neutral forum for offering differing ideas, and in seminars it does not occur often.

## DISAGREEING USING SUPPORTIVE FACEWORK

There are other moments when students agree minimally in order to disagree using supportive facework. In (2), Lucas states that the political situation in Antigua is "fine." He does not elaborate but invites a response by saying "you know what I mean?" This is a common phrase like "you know" but at the end of a turn in seminar it is an invitation to respond and Derek takes the invitation literally, focusing on that topic. Derek's comments are printed in full in (3), Chapter 6.

(2)

*Lucas*: Everything's fine they're doin– you know they're– they're– they're–
they've been doin this for years why– why throw a little ((makes a
sound)) in it.
Ya know what I mean?

*Derek*: She talks about that a lot when she talks about colonialism. And uh she
talks on page 36 . . . But I don't think that they're really in control of
their own lives. I think all of the things left by colonialism are still
there.

When Derek first responds to Lucas saying, "she talks about that a lot," he is giving face to Lucas by taking up his invitation to discuss this topic. A bit later he expresses his disagreement by referring indirectly to the view Lucas expressed, "they've been doing this for years," and contrasting it with his own saying, "I don't think that they're really in control of their own lives." Then he adds his main point, "I think all of the things left by colonialism are still there." By using "I think" he softens his disagreement. Although he disagrees with Lucas' position, he does not do that directly, so Lucas does not lose face. Derek also deepens the conversation by pointing out that systems of colonialism are still in place, which provides a reason why seemingly little has changed for the people.

This pattern of taking up the topic and then disagreeing is quite common. In another seminar we find a clear statement of partial agreement in (3). Joyce makes a comparison between two authors and then Sienna provides some facts before moving to disagree.

(3)

*Joyce*: But I don't– I– I never got from Martin Luther King that uh– um that same you know sort of air of superiority of the *high*ly educated and which I *do* get from Dubois=

*Sienna*: =Martin Luther King's whole um life work was trying– was attempting to– to *build* a movement [. . .] And so I think that you're very *right* they– they– they *did* um (.) have really different perspectives to– to offer on that. I think they were very– very um *diff*erent both a product of different times.

In (3) Sienna quickly intervenes to make a distinction between the work of Dubois and King, and then she shows solidarity to Joyce by agreeing that Dubois and King had different perspectives: "you're very right." These two examples of disagreements in (4) and (5), are similar in that they begin with factual information, but they are constructed differently, with Sienna using solidarity. Both Sienna and Derek use "I think" to soften the face threat of their disagreements. Why does Sienna also use solidarity by stating her agreement with Joyce but Derek does not? One reason may be that the nature of Sienna's disagreement was more severe and based on historical facts. She also moves the conversation from tone in Dubois' work to its goals, which adds to the conversation.

There are moments of humor around disagreements in seminars, some of which reinforce concepts being discussed and create an in-group sense of solidarity. In (4) everyone understands the humor because they have been discussing communities of practice and they have shared background knowledge. In this case, students are talking about virtual communities of practice based on gender. Evan questions the idea that gender practices would be understood in a virtual community.

(4)

*Evan*: We can talk about men and women in an abstract. You know we don't have meetings like everybody in one gender gets together and– and decides we feel a certain way about this. At least I don't think that happens.
((Lots of voices))

*Jerry*: Check your Twitter man
((Laughter))

Evan is making a humorous point about imagined communities of all men and all women gathering to agree on how they feel, and adds "at least I don't think that happens" as an added witticism. Jerry then tells him to check his Twitter account, where Evan may find just such a virtual community of practice. This is

**105**

a disagreement, but performed in a lighthearted way. The group builds solidarity by laughing together, reinforcing the ideas expressed and, at the same time, reinforcing their solidarity.

Students can be explicit in their disagreement even when their wording makes the disagreement indirect. One way to do this is to depersonalize it by not using *I* or *you*. In (5) Jan uses the phrase, "an argument" to depersonalize her disagreement and distance herself from the idea she is about to express. She lengthens her vowels as she is quickly turning pages in her book to the correct place and then she begins reading from the text.

(5)

| | |
|---|---|
| *Jan*: | Well I think an argument is they never did have a culture like o::n pa::ge thirty one she says [. . .] and I think that's the big thing is that they don't *have* culture like they don't have past. They don't have a land y'know like *slavery* is their past and their culture |
| | (2) |
| *Bart*: | So they do have a culture. |
| *Jan*: | Yeah but it's not their culture as– like I mean it *is* their culture but not like *nat*urally their culture I guess. |

Her depersonalized disagreement, "an argument is" saves face for herself and the student she is disagreeing with. Bart takes Jan's words to contradict her main point, and she has to amend her statement in order to save face. No doubt she also realized that her original statement was incorrect factually as well as theoretically. All societies have a culture.

Of course students can also be very explicit in their disagreement as Helen is in (6):

(6)

| | |
|---|---|
| *Helen*: | I disagree (.) like I think that um (.) I hear what you're saying [. . .] I feel like this is a book definitely with personal rage and I don't feel like it does represent the people of Antigua more—or represents me as the you and I don't know that that's necessarily her intention as to speak for anybody other than herself |

Using "I disagree" threatens the previous speaker's face because it is direct. However, Helen softens her statement with "I hear what you're saying." She indicates in this way that she can understand why he might have taken his position. Helen actually does not just disagree with the previous speaker but also with others. In particular, by adding "or represents me as the you," she is disagreeing with an earlier speaker who commented that Antiguans were reversing the gaze of the tourist and the colonizer, which had been very well received by students with several murmurs of appreciation. She speaks rapidly and possibly because she includes so many points of disagreement, more students enter the conversation and find ways to counter her points. This is a turning point in the conversation because Helen's disagreements stimulate new ideas and perspectives.

One of the resulting disagreements has no solidarity markers or hedges. In (7) Helen continues her line of disagreement by asking a rhetorical question. Zoe, who hadn't spoken yet, answers using another rhetorical question as an indirect disagreement.

(7)

*Helen*: Don't you then have a responsibility to go okay this is our past and where do we want our future to go=

*Zoe*: =Don't you also need access to the education to learn *how* to create a strong government?

*Paige*: And also if they don't have– if they don't have an experience with something else

We can see that Zoe's rhetorical question is understood as a disagreement because the next speaker, Paige, adds to Zoe's disagreement, "And also." Helen and Zoe are using "you" to refer to the society discussed in the text, so their rhetorical questions are impersonal and therefore not face threatening. Zoe and Paige's points are new and indicate a complexity beyond just voting, so they become part of the collaborative persuasive argument in this seminar.

## LOSING FACE IN FACTUAL DISAGREEMENTS

When a student is factually incorrect, others usually quickly disagree. In one seminar Scott proposes a definition of consciousness that he claims the author is suggesting. Molly says *I guess I didn't get that* and then she expands on her own interpretation of the author's point. By beginning her turn in this way, she softens her disagreement by focusing on *getting* the author's point. This metaphor of getting an idea highlights the usual way we understand reading: sometimes we get the point and sometimes we don't. Her phrase hides the underlying problem, that Scott was wrong about the author's point; as a result, Scott does not lose face with Molly's disagreement.

Perhaps because Molly's disagreement was subtle, Scott continues to elaborate on his idea of consciousness and two other students, Randy and Austin, step in to disagree with him, one after the other. Both softened their disagreements in different ways in order to indicate solidarity in (8), but they are more explicit than Molly:

(8)

*Randy*: See I still, I mean I think you're– beginning on page 59 is where he lists the– uh the features of consciousness. And he tries– he tends to describe them in some detail and he's pretty ambiguous in some cases admittedly. I– uh none of them seem to be awareness of your (1) [thought processes

*Austin*: [It seems to me that where we're getting stuck perhaps is in thinking with the idea of consciousness of being uh well I don't know how to say this but having to be conscious of yourself all the time. I don't think that's what he's saying. He's not saying that you have to be conscious of yourself and what you're thinking all the time. It's the fact that you have the ability to be introspective.

Both Randy and Austin introduce their disagreements in a way that softens their force. Randy gives face to Scott by saying, "he's pretty ambiguous in some cases admittedly," referring to the author. This allows Scott to have misunderstood some parts of the definition and it asserts common ground, that the author is not always clear. Austin introduces his disagreement with "It seems to me that where we're getting stuck perhaps," which indicates that they are all stuck, and share common ground. He uses the personal stance "it seems to me" and the hedge "perhaps" to soften his disagreement. Still, Austin contrasts what Scott claims the author is saying ("He's not saying that you have to be conscious of yourself") with what the author is actually saying. This is a clear and strong disagreement. Scott does not continue to push his interpretation and loses face.

What the author is saying is often in contention in seminars. In some cases, students do not soften or mitigate their disagreements. For example in another seminar, James makes an assertion about the author's conclusion that was challenged by Alex: "she doesn't say that." This is a direct disagreement, and although Alex speaks in a soft voice, it is clearly audible. James then turns to the text and tries to find some evidence for his view, beginning to read a couple of times and each time rejecting his choices. After holding the floor in this way for about 40 seconds, he says, "Ok well I can't find it. I don't know." (This incident shows that 40 seconds is actually a long time to hold the floor without having a point.) Alex then quotes evidence in the text that directly counters James' claim, and causes him to lose face. Another student helps James save face by saying, "It's just a general feeling that you get."

Although it is clear that James is wrong, the student supporting him gets additional support from other students with head nods. This disagreement comes in a particular context. Students are divided in groups by gender so these men are having their own conversation before joining the whole group. The faculty member divided the students by gender because the topic of the text was gender and conversation. These men were disagreeing with the author's ideas in part because they didn't believe their own interactions fit the author's description of what men do in conversations. They seemed to create a sense of solidarity based on their gender in this seminar in a joint rejection of the author's claims and that fleeting solidarity could have influenced the students to give James support even though it was clear that he was factually incorrect at this point and had no evidence for his point of view.

In a different seminar the disagreement is stronger because students challenge others for what they said and not what the author said. For example, in (9), Paul disputes Nick's assertion:

(9)
*Nick*:     Evolution is from simple to complex
*Paul*:     Not necessarily. Lizards evolved and maybe snakes evolved in a way that you could say from complex to simple because they're seeking out a niche [. . .] I think it's a fallacy to say that evolution is always simple to complex.

This is a direct disagreement in which Paul gives a counterexample, and then softens his disagreement by using an impersonal expression, *I think it's a fallacy to say*. This expression is less direct than using "you" or "your," but Paul causes Nick to lose face with his counterexample.

## USING ARGUMENTS TO WIN

Arguments to win are usually face threatening because the goal is win and not to give face to others. This is clearly the case in (10) when Amanda presents a face threat to Teri. She uses the phrase "he's talking about" to support Carlo's view, which is that barrio gangs are similar to little nations and to reject Teri's view that they are like any other organization, such as fraternities.

(10)
*Amanda*:   I think— I think this kind of little nation what he's talking about goes far beyond beyond frat boys. You're talking about little frat cliques— you're talking about gangs and cliques and I think he's talking about little *nations*. I mean completely separate. I'm talking
*Carlo*:                                                          [yeah
*Amanda*:   no cultural uh. No— nothing the same about their culture.
            the language is not the same. Not the same— nothing is the same. He's talking something com*pletely* different— he's not talking about little cliques and frat boys running around you're too fat I mean come on it's different.

> *Katie:* [ok let's talk about– let's talk about um China–
> Let's talk about Chinatown in San Francisco

Amanda uses a loud, sarcastic tone, a fast delivery, and a summarizing coda that ridicules: "I mean come on it's different." She also uses a lot of repetition. First, she repeats words that Carlo and Teri used in order to contrast them and to clarify the meaning of "little nations." Second, her near repetition of "nothing is the same" includes an example, "their language is not the same." Third, her repetition of little cliques includes frat boys possibly saying things like "you're too fat", which sharply contrasts with the physical activities of barrio gangs, the topic of this seminar. Clearly, disagreements can become heated and here Amanda is arguing to win. She gains authority by using sarcasm and repetition and she also causes Teri to lose face. Amanda has not deepened the conversation since she adds no new points except that fraternities and barrio gangs are culturally different, an obvious point. Katie moves to reduce the face threat by developing the notion of little nations in the last lines.

The next exchange took place early in the term and there were two student facilitators, a woman and a man. This seminar became centered on one student's ideas, Nick. Nick effectively holds the floor for 10 minutes by responding to each critique of his argument. (We saw another exchange with Nick in (9) above). He argues that because neurons change in the brain when humans learn something new, that humans pass along those changes to their offspring. Seven students and the faculty member disagree and point out the problem with his reasoning one by one, but he persists with his idea.

Nick is arguing to win. One strategy he uses is to respond to each critique by repeating what he has already said or adding information from his own thinking. In addition, he speaks loudly, and by leaning forward and laying his arms on the table, he creates a prominent space for himself. The pace was rapid and it was hard to get into the conversation. Note how one of the facilitators introduced his comments in (11):

(11)
> *Thomas:* Wait wait [. . .] you guys let me say a couple things [. . .] ok, first of all, and let me finish here. I think your idea is implausible and here's why [. . .]

Thomas gives a series of three imperatives to enter the conversation ("wait, let me, let me") and they are effective because he is allowed to speak without interruption. Another student explicitly indicates that two sides have been claimed when she says, "just for the sake of argument as a devil's advocate on Nick's side." This indicates that there is Nick's side and everyone else's.

Finally, there is the following exchange in (12), a climax in the argument that indicates very clearly that Nick believes he is right and everyone else is wrong. He uses *that's what I'm saying* to reinforce his point rather than explain it. FM is the faculty member.

(12)

| | |
|---|---|
| *Sally*: | Evolution is changing *struc*ture |
| *Nick*: | right that's what you're doing |
| *FM*: | wait |
| *Sally*: | =but i*deas* are not structure |
| *Nick*: | they *are* |
| ?: | no |
| *Nick*: | that's what I'm saying |
| *Sally*: | =I don't believe they're genetic structure. I don't believe that. |
| *Nick*: | =then you don't believe that the mind is what the brain does (derisive tone) |

This final phrase, "then you don't believe that the mind is what the brain does" has become the mantra of this class, so Nick is, in effect, arguing that because Sally doesn't accept his viewpoint, she is rejecting everything that they are learning. After a few more minutes, and interventions by the faculty member and facilitator, Nick realizes that no one wants to continue on his topic, and says, "We've run into a dead end because that's the one I've run into." This is a clear example of trying to save face. Nick uses "we" to indicate that everyone has been working on his idea rather than rejecting it and, by saying he also ran into a dead end, he's claiming that he's had the idea for a while.

## STUDENT PERSPECTIVES ON ARGUING TO WIN

In the last few minutes of the conversation about genetics, Thomas asks if anyone has points they want to raise. One student, Anita, who had not spoken during Nick's holding of the floor, says, "I felt that some people got run over in this seminar really bad." When asked to elaborate, she gave a strong critique without using Nick's name, saying that some people kept adhering to specific ideas in a stubborn way and she reports what Nick might have been thinking when she says, "This is my idea and I'm right and if you don't believe that then I'm going to keep yelling at your– whatever until you do believe it and I find that extremely offensive." She is not the author of this thought, she is just reporting it. This is an example of reported speech being used to depersonalize her comments and indirectly save face for Nick. She effectively categorizes Nick as someone who wants to win and is willing to threaten the face of others to do it.

Anita is sitting next to Nick, and he looks at her several times as she says this, but she addresses the group as a whole and does not glance his way. During Nick's argument with the group, she was clearly affected, putting her hands over her face and leaning back and at one point putting her head down on the table with her hands over it. Another woman then offers a suggestion that is also expressed as though Nick or another student was thinking these words, "we need to watch for when— If I'm not going to change my mind and I recognize that nobody else in the room is going to change their mind then— then that's a time to reevaluate the situation." Using reported speech allows her to suggest a different way for Nick to conduct himself in seminar. Sally then says, "I think we did that [. . .] maybe we could do it a little earlier." The laughter around the room indicates agreement with this point. Note that this last comment changes the "I" to "we" as a solidarity move indicating that everyone has responsibility for what goes on. Her statement also diffuses the situation.

Arguing to win indicates an underlying tension that many students new to college encounter: what is valid evidence in seminar? Although Nick draws on his personal experience, no one else supports his claims about the effects of experience on evolution. He does not seem to take into account the many clear explanations of how evolution works, even those by the faculty member. When he came to watch the playback of the conversation with me, Nick stated that this was a good seminar: "I just think that most people were able to get a better view of what was going on in the book rather than just saying this is right or this is wrong." Nick's inability to entertain other people's ideas was frustrating to several other students who came to see the playback of that seminar as we see in (13):

(13)
- Now that I look at it, I realize there was this huge conversation going on between like two or three people in the whole class, which is, I don't know, not really a discussion.
- Here's a problem when almost everyone thinks that one person is wrong factually. What do you do? Do you enlighten them without making it be intrusive or offensive to that person?
- Usually when we talk there's a mixed amount of people that are supporting one side or the other. It's kind of all focused on poor Nick here in that he's having to answer to a lot of these things rather than us having a discussion.

These comments indicate a common understanding of seminar as a conversation among all of the members. Although Nick was able to challenge the faculty member, present his own beliefs, and gain power by holding the floor, all of which are generally encouraged in seminars, he shaped his interaction based on arguing to win rather than arguing to persuade, as we can see by what students said at the end of seminar and in the playback sessions. In effect, he silenced other voices and students did not feel that they learned something valuable. He chose to present face threats to various students rather than showing respect for other ideas. Although he held the floor for 10 minutes in a two hour seminar, one student quoted in (13) only just realizes that Nick had monopolized the conversation as she watched the video playback. This indicates that students are busy in seminar trying to understand what others are saying, evaluating it, formulating what they might want to say, trying to find a way into the conversation, or trying to formulate an idea germinating in their minds. Consequently, they cannot always be counted on to help everyone see what is going on. That is the facilitator's job.

Nick's posture at the table, loud voice, and claims of authority all point to a masculine style. Researchers have found that men can be concerned with status in a group setting, and Nick laid claim to high status through his actions and words and he made a final statement designed to save his own face. Sally's approach of reasoning with Nick without raising her voice and her move towards solidarity at the end of seminar, "I think we did that [. . .] maybe we could do it a little earlier," points to a feminine style of cooperative behavior (Holmes, 1995). These styles are quite different in this case, but students do not use these styles at all times, and in fact, anyone can use a masculine or feminine style. In this seminar Nick positioned himself as having authority, but it is not the authority of a knowledgeable student that is highly valued in seminar; instead it is authority based on arguing to win. Sally positioned herself as a group member with responsibilities, reminding everyone of that value.

## CONCLUSION

Using supportive facework effectively during disagreements can help students create arguments to persuade, as Helen did in (6). Even though Helen introduces numerous points of disagreement all at once, she does not try to hold the floor continuously as Nick did. Other students were able to introduce new points and develop them into persuasive arguments. When conversations become heated, it can be hard for some students to avoid the strategies of arguing to win and use supportive facework. Both Amanda in (13) and Nick in (15) illustrated this form of argument, and it stalled the conversation rather than furthering it.

I have focused on disagreements in order to illustrate facework, which is always in play in conversations. It is important to point out that arguments do not need to be pervasive in seminars. Walter Ong (1981) points out that the tradition of argument in academia can be traced back to European medieval universities in which students were tested in combative oral presentations. Students were taught to take a stand or attack another student's stand rather than search for knowledge. The academic argument thus has a long tradition. We might contrast this long tradition with Peter Elbow's believing game, which I described in Chapter 6.

He points out that our first approach to new scholarship is looking for what is wrong with it. He recommends using "the believing game" as a heuristic device, not as a final goal because we need a way to discover the strengths of arguments that other scholars present.

## BEST PRACTICES

■ Disagreement is a central feature of seminars. Students and faculty members create a context with each seminar but, of course, they also bring their memory of past seminars and their own histories in the group. Many students report that they become more comfortable in the group as the academic term moves on. Students do not have to soften their disagreements using supportive facework, and in fact in one study of an MBA seminar, students expressed their disagreements more explicitly than in those I recorded: *You've got to look at it seriously though because; It's not true to say; I think you've got to look at; Didn't you feel that;* and *I think it's irrelevant that* (Basturkmen, 1999). The community of practice in each seminar will provide the context for how disagreements are phrased, and graduate programs can sometimes promote competition between students. What is important is to listen for the force of the disagreement given the context of the conversation. It may be helpful to introduce some examples of supportive facework.

■ It is useful to explain the difference between arguing to persuade and arguing to win, and to emphasize that if the point is learning, seminar should be an on-going exploration involving everyone. If a student appears to be arguing to win and not allowing others to enter the conversation, here are some ways facilitators can change the topic:

— *I'm not sure where this is going. I think we should move on.* This is an indirect way to suggest a change of topic.

— *I think it is time to stop and consider what is going on. Can anyone who has not been talking summarize what has been said?* By summarizing the ideas, students may be able to move from angry reactions to thinking about the ideas. This comment also underscores the fact that not many students have been participating in the conversation.

— *[to the student who won't cede the floor] I think you've explained your view clearly. I was interested by what [another student] said, and I wonder if we could develop that a little.* This is a segue into another topic that also gives face to the student who had a good idea.

— *[if a student has hurt feelings] Let's take a minute or two to discuss what just happened because feelings could be hurt.* Sometimes it's best to stop conversation to describe what you heard and refer to the covenant or rules. Whether or not students contribute at that moment is not as important as your pointing out what happened.

— *Actually, your idea seems to be X Theory. It was supported by [names] and discredited by [names] because.* Giving a clear framework for an idea or opinion can help students find more information after seminar. If the student's claim was not a specific theory, you can move to the theories in the text and ask how they might compare.

■ If you are interested in comparing "the doubting game" and "the believing game," you could divide your seminar into two groups and tell them they each need to come up with one or two arguments that either critique or extend the thesis of the text under consideration. Or, to make it a regular practice, you could assign an essay prior to seminar in which students would need to play one of those games each week.

■ If students try to paraphrase the point of disagreement, it is easier for everyone to follow what is going on. For example, students can preface their paraphrase with *what I think you're saying is.* This reformulation can focus the ideas being presented and allow good listeners to contribute usefully.

# Chapter 8

# Cross-Cultural Dynamics

In a sense we are often involved in cross-cultural dynamics and that is because we cannot know everyone's cultural background and how much it influences the way they talk. Even if someone has an accent, it can signal their origins in a different geographic region or another country, but not how acculturated they are. Besides accent, we categorize people according to race, ethnicity, gender, age, sexual orientation, and social class. We do this by observing the ways people look, talk, dress, behave, and value things. Importantly, we can overlook part of someone's identity because none of these classifications is clear cut. People can be ethnically or racially mixed, geographically dislocated, and their age, gender, and social class may not be immediately apparent.

Seminars are rich in cross-cultural dynamics, so one of the first questions we should address in thinking about teaching them is how to build tolerance for difference. I have often heard that seminars should be a safe place for students. To me, this means a number of things; for example, students of color should not feel singled out to speak for their racial or ethnic group; transgender students should be able to choose the pronoun of their choice (he or she or a neutral pronoun such as ze); everyone should respect the ideas and opinions of others; and regional and religious values should be tolerated. Seminars, however, are not always a safe place to test ideas, inform others of personal experience, or present arguments. Part of the reason is that we cannot know all of the possible individual and cultural triggers for our students or even ourselves, and part of the reason has to do with the nature of critical inquiry. We raise difficult problems in our classes and talking about those problems is not easy. In addition, we are not teaching in a vacuum. The social and political environments at the local, national, and global environments impact our teaching, and so does the climate at our own institutions.

A number of national debates contain labels or shorthand to delineate two sides, such as "a woman's choice" vs. "pro-life" and creationists vs. biologists. Some students refer to these debates in seminar and reveal received notions or heartfelt opinions based on their experiences. In addition, students may raise difficult questions about why race matters, the social construction of gender, and the history and current status of indigenous peoples. Questions like these are part of our social landscape and they can become important topics in seminars. When students take up these topics, they can raise awareness of the social identities in the room, and stereotypes can emerge, so facilitators need to be aware of what is going on. Sociolinguist James Paul Gee points out that our language practices have a political element. Politics has to do with how social goods are distributed as well as the values of the goods themselves (Gee, 2011). The social goods in seminar are the knowledge that students produce, the positions they take, the time spent on a topic, and the social capital that is stored or spent. Social goods are never fixed because the context in the conversation is always changing, but they are linked to ideologies. I am using ideology to refer to (usually) unconscious ways of understanding the world rather than only political ideologies such as progressive or conservative.

## THE GENDER BINARY

There are a host of ideologies that influence the ways we understand each other. Gender, for example, is sometimes conflated with biological sex, but in fact, it is a social and ideological construct, and there are different possibilities for gender display in different cultures. In the United States, gender is often regarded as a binary system in the media, in advertising, in government forms, and in families. The gender binary is based on stereotypical notions of what it means to be a woman or a man although the Lesbian, Gay, Bisexual, Transsexual, Queer/Questioning (LGBTQ) community is now more widely acknowledged. The binary ideology is based on gendered practices that can be found in all of our institutions (e.g., education, government, religion, the family) and in our daily activities. For example, in a team-taught class called Gender Performances, my colleague asked students to bring their deodorants to class and we classified most of them as being designed for men or women, with a very small number being gender neutral. Just a glance at the shelves in a store reveals that deodorant containers with pink and other pastels are for women; red, black, and other dark colors are for men. The product descriptions and instructions for use were also starkly different, with those for men being briefer and more focused on basic use of the product than women's products. In our interdisciplinary class combining sociolinguistics and sociology, we gave students field assignments to examine children's toys, clothing, greeting cards, people's nonverbal behavior, and conversations. Our students found clear evidence each week that the products we buy, the ways we interact, and the ways we negotiate our worlds are influenced by a gendered, binary understanding of difference.

As the central symbolic system in our worlds, language is a primary way to maintain and contest the gender binary. This may be a major reason that Deborah Tannen's (1990) *You just don't understand: Women and men in conversation,* was on the best-seller list for nearly four years. She argues that because boys and girls are socialized in different ways, they use language differently. Men use conversation to establish hierarchy and independence; women use language to establish intimacy and social networks. Men often focus on independence, and they are more oriented to public display of that information. Women focus on intimacy and they are more focused on the social aspects of language. She argues that a cultural difference exists between the two genders and so we need to understand the two ways of talking to minimize misunderstandings. These differences are related to power so many of her findings are useful to consider in seminars.

Language and gender researchers do not claim that all men speak one way and all women speak another way. The context of the conversation can change the ways that people interact and the social identities that we perform can also play a role. In seminars, for example, I have not found many differences in the ways men and women talk, but it is important to recognize that there is at least one continuum for gendered styles of speaking with a masculine style at one end and a feminine style at the other. I referred to this continuum in Chapter 7 in my discussion of arguments to win. These styles are related to stereotypical notions of what men and women should be like. Men's voices are deeper and louder; they gain power in the conversation by introducing topics and sustaining topics they find important; they tell jokes; they are less polite and more likely to use profanity. Women's voices are higher and weaker; they voice their ideas less assertively, they are more polite and cooperative; and they don't use profanity. By imagining a continuum with these stereotypes at either end, we can see that some people may use a more masculine or a more feminine style.

## INTERACTIONS OF GENDER, IDENTITIES, AND STYLE

Importantly, we are not defined by our gender; instead we construct our gender and all other aspects of our identities by the ways we behave, dress, speak, and by the activities we engage in every moment of every day. Identity is a process that we continually produce in all of our conversations; it is not something that we achieve and possess. Although gender identity is a major factor in our presentation of self, it is tied to all of our other social identities. The concept of intersectionality (Collins, 1993), the intersections between race, gender, and social class, is important to keep in mind, particularly when we think about social and economic power. In seminars, speakers gain power by making a good point or contributing a new idea, and they also lay claim to social goods. One of these goods has to do with determining the terminology being used. In a seminar discussing a famous female scientist, for example, Jacinta announces two aspects of her identity in order to make her authority clear: she would prefer students not use the term "minority" in (1):

(1)

*Andrew*: Some think that a lot of new discovery you know particularly I guess in science is being able to uh identify opportunity ↑ Do at least in this day and age maybe because of things that we're all up against do women and minorities see more opportunities out there than non-women and non-minorities ↑

*Jacinta*: well you know what I hate to do this to you but you know when you say women and minorities I am a woman and I'm not a minority I'm sorry ((laughs))

*Andrew*: [I'm using

*Jacinta*: I know but– but I mean– I mean I'm not like trying to like tell you how to talk but for me personally that's– I'm a woman and a person of color but if you look up the word minority in the dictionary I mean ( ) But see– I– I just like– don't like to categorize me as just as a minority because I am also a woman

*Andrew*: uh hum

*Jacinta*: so I don't know where that comes from ( )

*Sydney*: [it comes from political

*Jacinta*: yeah but see I'm just saying ( ) I'm not trying to get into a discussion just in that– next time if you use that if you *could*

*Andrew*: [oh ok ((nods))

*Jacinta*: you know to use that

Jacinta wants students to use "people of color" rather than "a minority." She also points out the importance of intertextuality; in this case, designating both gender and race. She uses lots of hedges, "I hate to do this to you," "I mean I'm not like trying to like tell you how to talk," and "I'm just saying" to soften the disagreement she has with Andrew's use of "minority." By speaking up about terminology, Jacinta gains power because even if she says she is not trying to tell Andrew how to talk, she is doing just that. Her authority comes from her own experience and her self-identification as a woman of color.

Besides these gendered styles and the intersections of race and ethnicity, it is useful to consider styles, and how students use them position themselves and others. In seminar, students position themselves on a number of continua: authority ⟷ not an authority; articulate ⟷ inarticulate; talker ⟷ silent; formal ⟷ informal; powerful ⟷ powerless; direct ⟷ indirect; in solidarity ⟷ at a distance. Although this positioning can be momentary, students may develop their styles based on these continua over time.

Positioning is not independent of our social worlds, of course. We are constrained by social expectations and our own understanding of gender performance. Another way to look at how men and women position themselves in seminar is to examine the cultural models that students use. Cultural models are cognitive schemas or simplified theories that we use to quickly understand and make sense of the world. They provide a cognitive organization that frames experience and supplies interpretations of that experience (Holland & Quinn, 1987). We have models of seminar, marriage, and baseball games in our minds. These models do not usually match actual events in our lives. In Chapter 1, I sketched the cultural model of a seminar most of us have as being "a reasoned, articulate conversation including thoughtful questions where learning is evident in 'ah hah' moments." However, a major reason for reading this book is that seminars do not always conform to this model.

## A GENDERED WAY OF UNDERSTANDING SEMINARS

To investigate the cultural model of seminars, I examined metaphors students use to describe them. My original goal was to see if those metaphors changed from the fall term to spring. I recorded 36 students' comments (20 women and 16 men) as they watched edited versions of their videotaped seminars (Fiksdal, 2008). As I listed metaphors, I began to see gender differences in the ways they were worded. I found 371 metaphors which I categorized into 10 metaphor clusters: LANGUAGE IS A CONDUIT, IDEAS ARE THROWABLE OBJECTS, IDEAS ARE MALLEABLE OBJECTS, IDEAS ARE VALUABLE OBJECTS, SEMINAR IS A JOURNEY, SEMINAR IS A BUILDING, SEMINAR IS A MACHINE, SEMINAR IS WAR, SEMINAR IS A CONTAINER, SEMINAR IS A FLOW. I discussed some of these metaphors in Chapter 5 to reveal how students' conception of seminar can impact their interactions. At this point we will examine how students phrase these metaphors because we find subtle differences. Men and women use the same metaphors in each of these clusters and their metaphors reveal a cultural model of collaborative seminar discourse. Both men and women see students working together and moving toward a common goal; however, the metaphorical expressions they use construct a relationship between the self and other that is different in intriguing ways.

Men indicate the relationship with self and other in their metaphors that reveals an underlying metaphor, SEMINAR IS A GAME. It entails having a clearly defined goal, collaboration, competition, rules, winning, and losing. Speakers have some control over the game and therefore men's metaphors reveal an agent moving, carrying, manipulating ideas. Men talk about others and themselves as agents. In contrast, the metaphors women use do not fit easily into the game metaphor; instead, they indicate the relationship between self and other as SEMINAR IS A COMMUNITY. This entails sharing, valuing, and helping other seminar members. The goal is collaboration with others. Women used *we* and collective *you* quite often: individual actors are important only if they are helping. It is the group or collective that is salient.

Examples of metaphors students used will help clarify this distinction. In the IDEAS ARE THROWABLE OBJECTS metaphor cluster, a man speaks of throwing ideas as though they are balls in (2). Throwing ideas focuses the conversation on individual students.

(2)
I also talk with him a lot outside of class and in a way it's like a seminar because, I mean, I throw lots of ideas at him.

I only found one woman who used this metaphor. Unlike the men, she explicitly refers to a game of footwork that everyone is playing as a way of testing them so that the group could present them in (3):

(3)
I was thinking that we were using that footwork kind of idea, tossing it around just to see how it would work before we presented it, 'cause it's kind of a good idea to test your ideas before you present them to somebody else.

Her formulation of the IDEAS ARE THROWABLE OBJECTS metaphor as useful for the group has to do with testing ideas before presenting them. This contrasts with (2) where the individual's act of tossing or throwing ideas is a tactic that may be understood to be valuable in itself at times.

As we saw in Chapter 5, the most common metaphors fell in the category SEMINAR IS A JOURNEY. When we examine how these metaphors are composed differently by men and women, we see that men usually commented on the behavior of other people, or, if they spoke of themselves, it was to explain their actions as an agent as in (4) and (5). All of these metaphors are about tangents or being off the journey's path.

(4) People lose sight of the goal and stray.
(5) When others go off on tangents or get off the subject, then I go into my prosecutor mode.

Women used *we* and if not, they focus on the community as in (6) and (7):

(6) We have this tendency to go off on this tangent.
(7) Someone will kind of get off on a tangent which is ok, but then you'll kind of lose some people, at least some people's interest.

The second most common metaphor for seminars was SEMINAR IS A BUILDING. The contrast between (8), which is by a man and focuses on *I*; and (9), which is by a woman and focuses on *we*, was a noticeable pattern:

(8) It is a place to build on my ideas.
(9) We got more and more information built on each other which was good.

Importantly, both of these conceptual metaphors—SEMINAR IS A GAME and SEMINAR IS A COMMUNITY—entail collaboration and communication and they are both part of the cultural model of collaboration in seminars. This cultural model of conversation emerges from a community of practice. That is, students hear about seminars from faculty and other students, engage in them every week, discuss their seminars with friends, and move from being peripheral observers to full-fledged members of the seminar. They commit to collaborative learning and they share practices of framing their ideas in particular ways in order to convey their ideas but also to communicate identities, power, face, and solidarity. Although men and women may have slightly different cultural models for describing seminar, in the conversations themselves, their gender identities can become less salient in some situations depending on the topic, the people involved, and the goals of the conversation.

The primary goal of seminar is collaborative learning, so one value, or social good, is hearing from as many students as possible in order to hear their perspectives and weigh their value. Analyzing a large corpus of discussions in university classrooms, Schleef (2008) found that there were no significant gender differences because, he argued, of the demands of academic discourse. He found that when the information flow was disrupted it was women who moved to supply information to help others out while men made no effort to do so. I have not noticed this difference in seminars; instead, I find that those who are more prepared are the ones who help out with information such as what the author stated or where others can find the information they are searching for. Not all moves to help are equal, and, depending on one's gender and status in seminar, they can be interpreted as a competitive action. In one instance, for example, there was an incident that indicated providing information can be interpreted as a challenge. Jason was making a point and remarked that he wished he had the book from the week before so he could find the passage he was referring to. Tony, who was sitting half way around the room, then passed the book to him. Jason told me in the video playback session that Tony's action made him really angry. He wasn't sure what Tony's intentions were, but he saw his actions as a challenge. I noted that Jason did not open the book to look for the passage. In this case, if Jason was conceptualizing seminar as a game, then he was analyzing Tony's motives for passing the book because it caused him to lose face.

**123**

When I have asked students in my classes to interview other students about gender differences, most students say that they notice individual differences more than gender differences. But a few interviews pointed to differences I have also noticed in my teaching. One male student said, "Men are more dominant when there is a disagreement." I am not sure what the student means by dominant, but I have noticed that men often take longer turns in disagreements. In another interview, a student commented in detail about one specific man in his seminar (10):

(10)
*Chaz*:  Another thing is the volume in voice too and depth uh and the question pattern too so it's like wit– uh Ed who is one of the four guys in my class he will talk and it will be a thunderous like I've got something to say and I'm gonna tell you this like thing and then the women's pattern is more like Do you know what we want to do? You know like more of like this question pattern rather than a deep like it's scary. I don't even want to listen to Ed anymore cuz it's terrifying. ((laughs))

Chaz describes Ed as positioning himself with authority by using a deep, loud voice and announcing what he wants to say. He uses reported speech, "I've got something to say and I'm gonna tell you this" to vividly describe how Ed talks. He contrasts that style with introducing questions and he says it is women who do that. Another student points out that men make closed statements but women do not make as many. Ed's comments are an example of closed statements and they may not invite comments from others.

Not all students thought men were the dominant speakers; some felt that women were. Quite often students pointed out other ways students positioned themselves that seemed more important than gender: as flirts, smart, pretentious, talkative, and quiet. These were very brief interviews focused primarily on how the interviewees interacted in seminar, but they show that how students perceive gender as a factor in seminar is quite varied.

## GENDER AND AUTHORITY

The connections between gender and how one positions oneself as an authority needs much more study, but recent research indicates that even the way we produce our speech can be gendered. Women use creaky voice, also called vocal fry, much more than men. Creaky voice is an effect produced by vibration of the vocal chords at just one end, so sound comes through, but it sounds raspy. One way to produce it is to pronounce "button" without pronouncing the "t." The sound you produce instead of the "t" can be prolonged, and that is creaky voice. Recent research has shown that people hear it and believe that the speakers are knowledgeable and educated (Yuasa, 2010). Some researchers hypothesize that young women may use it to sound more authoritative because it lowers the pitch of their voices. It is not used in every word, but it can be used for a phrase or a speaker's turn such as "yeah I think I've heard of that" (Yuasa, 2010, p. 326). Its rapid spread coincides with another phenomenon, and that is a lowering of pitch in women's voices in comparison with fifty years ago. The lowering of voice pitch is significant in thinking about how women position themselves, because, generally speaking, men have lower voices and, generally, more political and social power than women.

Another variable that could be studied to see if it affects the ways men and women talk in seminar is the gender of the faculty member who is facilitating. In my data male students sometimes challenge the authority of male faculty members. This occurred in two seminars I recorded, and in both it was the authority of the faculty member that was questioned. I report on one in (11). The topic of the conversation is awareness during dreams. Taylor disagrees with the faculty member, who wrote a question on the board, as did all of the students. When the faculty member took a turn in the conversation, he explained his question by saying that there were two conflicting views in the reading that he had been considering. Taylor does not agree and states that directly.

(11)

*Taylor*: I disagree that there's a conflict between those views. For two reasons. One. ((laughter from others)) First of all if you recall when you're talking about the action is the key ((points to the board)) they're referring to you being in a dream and where you let the– how the dream be played take its course of events and not try and interpret the symbolic meanings of the elements in the dream. So they're saying that what your– your action has done in that dream and ( ) there's some positive benefit is– is– is– makes no difference in what a certain person means within their dream. Whereas the second one ((points to board)) talk don't fight is talking where you're in a uh hostile dream situation and you're being at*tacked*. Those are two *to*tally separate instances. And my *sec*ond point is. Even if they *were* the same instances talking *is* an action so therefore you *are* taking an action regardless of what you do whether it's a physical action or a verbal action.

Taylor provided a point by point disagreement. When he finished, the faculty member looked at him and nodded a little while smiling. He did not respond, probably because another student signaled that he wanted to speak. The students held a ball of string as they spoke, and passed or threw it to the next speaker.

In another study (Rees-Miller, 2000, p. 1093) a faculty member is challenged indirectly by a male student in (12) when discussing the book *Strategies of slaves and women*:

(12)
*Earl*:   What do you– what do you know about this author?
*Prof*:   [Gives information on where the author teaches.] She's wonderful. That's a good question. [Gives information on what the author has written.] It's a fair question. It's an interesting question.

The professor understands Earl's question as a disagreement, giving three positive comments about his question. Later, Earl brings up his disagreement three more times in (13). Ellipses points mark the three contributions.

(13)
*Earl*:   I think that's a major drawback of the book. There's no context [. . .] no other factors they talk about . . . This book concentrates on the women so it's slanted. We don't know about the men . . . That's why I don't like the book. [. . . It's] only the story of six people.

In the three classes Rees-Miller observed, disagreements with the professor were softened about half the time, and the professors softened their disagreements with students over three quarters of the time. In (11) and (12) we do not see any disagreement from faculty members even though in (11) the faculty member's analysis of the text is directly challenged, and in (12) the choice of text for class is challenged.

In my experience, students have challenged the choice of a text as in (12) or (13), but I have not heard stronger disagreements or direct resistance with the on-going work in class as in (11). This could be due to my gender, teaching style, or other factors such as amounts of jockeying for status. I did not find challenges directed to the faculty member by female or transgender students in my data or in research on seminars, but colleagues confirm that this can and does happen.

## CHALLENGES IN GAINING AUTHORITY

Besides gender, students are grappling with a new identity of "college student learning to use academic discourse." In my experience, most students new to my college are learning to use academic discourse in seminars for the first time, so they are more likely to use conversational styles from other parts of their lives, such as everyday conversation among friends or co-workers and classroom discussions in high schools. They take a stance that is authoritative at times to get their point across, but they may also take this stance because they believe it is expected. Students position themselves as knowers or idea generators or humorists depending on the circumstances such as how well they read and understood the text, and how confident they are of others accepting their opinions. Their identities from high school and work settings gradually become less important over time because in seminar they have a new community of practice where they are evaluated on the merits of their thinking, collaboration, and expression. For all students, this change of using conversation to learn collaboratively creates a major challenge. They have the opportunity to reinvent their identities because they have joined a new community of practice, and, of course, some consciously forge new identities in college. As they explore this new way of approaching texts and as they adapt to academic approaches to inquiry, students can feel vulnerable. They hear and evaluate perspectives that challenge them in many ways.

One of the major challenges in seminar is to help students understand that everyone's perspectives matter. Some have come from relatively homogenous cultures, and many do not know how to talk about major issues involving race, class, and gender. In addition, students from minoritized groups (Sensoy & DiAngelo, 2012) may not feel comfortable speaking about these topics either. (These groups are devalued in society and that process is captured by this term.) In a study of minoritized students in their first semester of college, John Wesley White followed four students closely, meeting with them on several occasions. He found that they did not feel comfortable expressing their ideas in class because they did not want to be seen as speaking for their cultural group, they did not want to stand out especially in discussions about race or issues that directly affect race, and they were not fluent in academic discourse. Maria, a student in White's study, says, *why should they [students and professors] listen to me? Why should I say anything if, because of, like, how I say it, I'm not gonna be taken seriously* (2011, pp. 256–257)? Another issue for these students was not having the knowledge that others seemed to already have. They all mentioned this problem, and it may be heightened for some African-American students.

In African-American culture, there are a number of practices that are highly valued. One is to have a cool face; that is, to be calm and detached yet in control. In conversation it is important to use eloquence and precise timing. African-Americans can lose this cool face by not knowing meanings of particular words or the working of particular systems (Morgan, 2010). Being worried about not having the same level of knowledge as other students can silence minoritized students as can not wanting to "sound white." Changing the ways they interact in seminar may make them feel that they are giving up part of their social identity. In fact, however, being able to speak in different ways is something that we all know how to do. When we talk to babies and small children, we usually raise our voices and use very simple vocabulary. When we talk to family and friends we do not use the academic discourse we use in the classroom. When we are at work, we use specialized vocabulary. These ways of talking were discussed in

**127**

Chapter 3, and the term "registers" was introduced to describe them. Faculty members and students who speak nonstandard dialects often learn to code-switch. That is, they use different dialects and styles in different situations. Students can be unfamiliar with this practice and not realize that they are adding to their linguistic repertoire rather than giving up parts of themselves when they use academic discourse.

## MICROAGGRESSIONS

Bias against students of color, those who identify as lesbian, gay, bisexual, or transgender or questioning/queer (LGBTQ) is well researched in social psychology. The ways that bias can occur can be overt or subtle, but here we will focus on microaggressions. These are subtle slights and insults that privileged speakers may not be aware of (Sue, 2010; Sue et al., 2007). Denying that prejudice exists is a microaggression for some students in my seminars, for example, because they experience it often and microaggressions detract from the learning process. One survey of graduate and undergraduate students in a large university found that everyone, faculty and students of color alike, experienced far more subtle bias than overt bias over a year's time with 34% of undergraduates reporting being a target of microagression. The most frequent type was based on sex (36%), followed by race or ethnicity (19%). Undergraduates perceived more overt and subtle forms of bias in the classroom than did instructors. Students also perceived instructors as occasional sources of bias in the classroom (Boysen, Vogel, Cope, & Hubbard, 2009).

I list a few examples of microaggression that I extracted from Portman, Bui, Ogaz, Treviño (2009) in (14):

(14)
- *Today we are going to have a debate on immigration. I expect the three Latino students and a few of you to argue in favor of immigration. The rest of you will provide arguments against immigration.*
- *I've eaten and shopped plenty of times in West Denver and it's nothing like you describe it. How long have you lived there and who are you hanging out with?*
- *For the class project, I want you to think about a romantic relationship that you have had with a member of the opposite sex. Think and write about your observations.*
- *For this class, you are required to visit four art galleries located in the downtown area. The entrance fees vary but I am sure you can afford it.*
- *If you are Native American, I don't want you to write your paper on Native Americans. You already know everything about that group and besides you will be biased in your writing.*
- *I am inviting you all over to my house for dinner after class next week to discuss your projects. Ali, I know its Ramadan, but hope you'll join us anyway.*

- *If anyone has a disability, raise your hand right now so that we can make special accommodations for you.*

In each of these microaggressions, the faculty member is making assumptions from a white or middle class or able or heterosexual point of view. And, in some cases, the faculty member is making assumptions about what students know because they are a member of a particular cultural group. In seminar students can also make similar sorts of comments, or make assumptions based on race, gender, class, disability, age, or sexual orientation. To avoid hearing microaggressions, some students choose to pass for the dominant group in the room by not revealing some aspects of their social identities. For example, an African-American student of mine in an intensive discourse analysis class did not reveal that he spoke African-American English Vernacular (AAVE). This class focused on language variation and various dialects including AAVE. After the class had ended, his closest friend in class told me of his fluency in AAVE. During class, then, he passed as a speaker of mainstream English when we discussed the structure and functions of AAVE. By not revealing himself as a speaker of this dialect, he avoided being the only representative of AAVE speakers who might have to speak for all such speakers.

Another way that microaggression can occur is in discussing racism. This is due partly to the fact that discussions of racism are often avoided and white students and faculty do not always know how to approach the topic, and partly because racism is still present in our culture. Research shows that people positioning themselves as progressives in conversations assume that it is common sense not to be racist. Racists are others. One way this othering can be done is to use reported speech because in reported speech, the speaker is reporting on someone else's speech and using their intonation and words rather than the speaker's. It disassociates the speaker from the other, and allows for an evaluation of the racist other. Benwell (2012, p. 362) discusses what he terms common sense anti-racism in the British context and cites a speaker using reported speech: "ooh you know the sort of classic they come to our country they should be like us." Using "you know" is a way of indicating that the speaker and the listener are on common ground—both know about this often heard classic comment, "they come to our country they should be like us." By presenting views of racism in this common sense framework, any discussion is avoided.

Besides attributing racism to others, whites use certain phrases to avoid talking about racism. For example, a sociologist argues that color blind racism is a central ideology of the post-civil rights era that permeates discourse about race by whites (Bonilla-Silva, 2002). He analyzed interviews of university students talking about race outside of class. The phrase that he found most students use is, *I'm not prejudiced but*. I recognize this phrase and have heard it in a number of forms: *I'm not homophobic but* or *I'm not sexist but*. This is a way that some students introduce controversial topics in seminar. The words coming after the conjunction, *but*, identify the speaker as exactly what he or she claims not to be. Sometimes we can accept the comments at face value, but they can also be hurtful. Another phrase Bonilla-Silva found, *some of my best friends are black/Hispanic/Asian/gay but*, prefaces a biased statement. The statement positions the speaker as not prejudiced, but the next words indicate prejudice all the same.

In a seminar where there was a focus on one student's argument to win, described in Chapter 7, Nick makes an argument that there is a racism gene, even though students and the faculty member pointed out the fallacy of his argument. Their disagreement may have led to his controversial statement in (15) because he is energized, speaking loudly, and using his hands to punctuate his points:

(15)

*Nick:*   I find nothing wrong with racism. And that's because my family comes from Texas. And for eons back. And then from *Germ*any. And they believe racism is the way to live ((accented by hand chopping down with each phrase)). I was not taught that in my household. But I believed that until I was four or five. And then it took a lot of decision making on my part to decide differently.

In this rather confused statement, Nick is asserting that his family, though apparently not his immediate family, is racist and that that is normal because they live in Texas. His first statement, "I find nothing wrong with racism" immediately quiets the students, some of whom had been talking quietly among themselves about his previous assertions. He does not explain this comment, but his rhetorical strategy seems to be that for these racist others (his extended family), being racist is completely normal. We infer from his comments that he is not like them. Anita, who is sitting next to Nick, covers her face with her hands during this part of the conversation.

In (15), it is others who are racist and Nick places an emphasis on the habitual nature of being racist. Most often in the "racists are others" comments there is also an evaluation indicating that being racist in this way is terrible. In Nick's case, he was arguing that there is a racist gene, so one can infer that his family should not really receive any blame. Although he sought to distance himself from being a racist, his first statement, *I find nothing wrong with racism*, continues to resonate with other students and they enter the conversation to dispute his view about genetic inheritance. As I pointed out in Chapter 7, Anita characterized this and Nick's other controversial statements by using reported speech of what was going through Nick's mind: "This is my idea and I'm right and if you don't believe that then I'm going to keep yelling at your– whatever until you do believe it and I find that extremely offensive."

## SILENCING AND BEING SILENCED

Unlike Anita, some students are silenced by biased talk, and they do not feel comfortable pointing it out. In Anita's case, the student facilitator asked if there were any other issues they should discuss, so she had the opportunity to explain why she was so offended by Nick's argument. Still, it took courage to do so since she was sitting next to him and he was a powerful presence in the room with his extended argument to win, his loud voice, use of sharp hand gestures, and a body posture that used more space than other students. Unless the facilitator creates a time for a discussion of a microaggression, students do not always voice their concerns.

In a seminar I discussed in Chapter 6, a student apparently felt that the conversation excluded him because, in a playback session, he commented that it was a "feminar" and he had almost left the room. He did not voice his concern in that seminar or to his faculty member. In my experience, students are increasingly more likely to comment on microaggressions whether or not they feel personally attacked than in the past. Still, I hear from students after class about feeling hurt by the way another student phrased their comments, or used a social group as an example for a stereotyped assessment. Also, sometimes students hear a comment in a very different way than it was intended. The fact that our words do not linger in time means that we can have very different perceptions of precisely what someone said and what they meant. It is very difficult to create a safe environment and students can feel silenced.

Being silenced can result from many conversational practices. Using *men and women* to mean all adults, for example, underscores the gender binary. Interrogating binary gender roles can happen if students feel safe. Blackburn and Clark report on discussions of literature about the lesbian, gay, bi-sexual, transsexual, and queer or questioning (LGBTQ) community that they conducted for three years with a small group of LGBTQ and straight adolescents and young adults in a youth center. In (16) a student wonders whether an experience is the same for LGBTQ people as for straight people (Blackburn & Clark, 2011, p. 239):

(16)
*Mollie*: I'm interested in the idea of everybody living double lives thing, because I do think, because I agree when you [Rebecca] are saying that, I'm thinking, "Oh, yeah, yeah, yeah, I agree." And then you [Liz] say, "It's different. It's more intense," I agree [. . .] And I'm trying to figure out what feels different to me about it, like something about more like fear based or protection oriented or something.

Mollie is discussing athletics and focuses on the importance of protection as one aspect of the difference members of the LGBTQ community experience.

As Blackburn and Clark point out, heteronormativity can occur in conversations of the LGBTQ community. In (17) they provide an example of a discussion on the novel *Boy meets boy* (Blackburn & Clark, 2011, p 236):

(17)

*Mary*: And I like [LGBTQ-themed books], be-cause they're just like straight books except for they have gay characters or like gay/lesbian/bisexual characters.

*Shelby*: Yeah, that's one of the things I noticed a lot, too, is that I'm straight reading this book. And because the narrator was male, you know, it was a book about homosexuals, but it could have just as easily been a female. I didn't really notice any difference, you know. It wasn't challenging for me to sympathize with the love story, because it didn't really make a difference whether or not it was a boy.

Both Mary and Shelby are straight, so one might expect them to generalize the experiences of characters in these novels, but they are not the only group members who expressed this idea. A young gay man often remarked, "We've all been there and everyone has felt that way before," in describing a feeling or experience of one of the gay or lesbian characters. Blackburn and Clark theorize that these are strategies he learned by being openly gay since middle school and encountering many homophobic situations. Universalizing themes rather than pointing out differences in lesbian and gay characters could be a self-protective move he had often made in class discussions.

In my seminars, I have heard students refer to their partners, and this term masks more gendered terms. Students have announced their preferred pronoun so that the ambiguity of their appearance and voice would be clarified. Others have come out of the closet in seminars, and some have announced their affiliation with the LGBTQ community. Leap, an anthropologist, points out that if the closet is part of gay culture, then then the closet has a language that privileges silence over speech, concealment over cooperation, and safety over risk (1999, p. 268). Understanding when to speak and when to remain silent is part of what students learn as members of the LGBTQ community.

Silence can also be a choice for students who are not native speakers of English. One researcher interviewed Japanese students about interaction in seminars at an Australian university, and one said, "Not so many Australians are shy, I think [. . .] compared with Asian people who are shy, they are somehow totally different [. . .] Even if they are shy, they would give their opinions" (Nakane, 2006, p. 1818). The Japanese students did not want to speak in seminars for fear of being wrong and their faculty members saw their silent behavior as both being shy and not being strong students. Giving opinions, right or wrong, is a value in Australian universities, as in the United States, because the negotiation of ideas is at the center of learning and it is important to develop a voice. As we have seen, offering ideas in seminar is risky for many students, but it is important to realize that different cultural models of education lead to very different behaviors in seminar. In my own teaching I have had many Japanese students in my classes, and they have explained that spontaneous expression of ideas is difficult. They would prefer having a list of questions that they can prepare prior to class so that they can speak with confidence. This is a useful practice for all students.

## CONCLUSION

In order for collaborative learning to occur effectively, every student needs to actively cultivate a voice and yet social identities can inhibit students from talking. We need to raise awareness of silencing behaviors. Microaggressions, positioning others by labeling identity, universalizing experience, assuming students are comfortable with their silence—all are important to address in teaching effective seminars. Gender socialization and ideologies can influence the ways we think about seminar. In addition, gender is just one of our social identities and we perform these identities in various ways and at various times in conversations. Considering the cross-cultural dynamics of each seminar group, both spoken and unspoken, can help you choose approaches that encourage every student to participate. Seminars may not always be safe, but they can be times for deep learning about cultural and social differences.

## BEST PRACTICES

■ Students report that instructors who were comfortable discussing diversity issues and who provided support and validation of students' experiences were most effective (Sue et al., 2007). These instructors tended to directly address diversity, accept race as a legitimate topic, and validate all students' experiences. My colleague, José Gómez, says that in his experience, students bring up ideas that may be homophobic, racist, or sexist without addressing another student. Not all students may have the same level of understanding of these issues, so he usually waits for a break and then addresses hurtful comments without referring to the student who made the statement; instead he discusses the issues. If a student repeatedly uses microaggressions, he speaks to that student outside of seminar.

■ If the topic of the reading is race or racism, then according to my colleague, George Freeman, it can be useful to divide into self-selecting caucus groups. Students can choose if they want to join other students of color, for example, and the types of groups will emerge from conversations among the students. Caucuses can be useful for students of color who have confronted racism and white privilege and want to talk openly about it. For white students who are just beginning to understand the issues, caucuses with students who are at the same level of understanding can also be helpful. Caucuses allow students a forum to state their views openly, and then when the groups merge for the whole group seminar, allies are established for possibly difficult conversations.

■ If it is appropriate in your class, having conversations about racism can be very helpful. My colleague, Toska Olson, recommends using metaphors to encourage students to take part in the conversation: *we're just tossing out ideas, all of us can play devil's advocate*, and *we can evaluate ideas without evaluating the person who put them out there.* This might be most effective if students have some readings about prejudice, stereotypes, and racism. I have found the following texts to be very useful: Sensoy and DiAngelo (2012), *Is everybody equal: An introduction of key concepts in social justice education;* Tatum (2003), *"Why are all the black kids sitting together in the cafeteria?"* and Johnson (2006) *Privilege, power, and difference.*

■ Facilitators can explain how to be an ally of a minoritized group of the LGBTQ community so that students from those groups feel included. Learning the ways people want to be identified is important, because students have the right to the labels they prefer. Reflecting on how to reduce prejudice in conversations, speaking out against it, and questioning stereotypes are useful. Speaking for minoritized students is not helpful; instead, providing support for their points of view can be. Some useful Internet resources are listed on the website for this book.

■ Elizabeth Morrish (2002) points out that heterosexual faculty members may find it perfectly acceptable to refer to their marital status in class, but she tries to avoid pronouns that would identify her as a lesbian. She referred to her partner's pronunciation by saying, "that's a standard Mid-Western pronunciation" rather than, "she has." Morrish points out that her avoidance of "she" signals to the gay and lesbian students that she is a lesbian, but other students may not notice it.

■ Because some students are not comfortable speaking in seminar, assessing how much they participate should not be the only measure of what they are doing in seminar. Besides small group work and round robins at the end of seminar as suggested in Chapter 2, students can write one-paragraph summaries of what they learned in seminar and post it to the class website. Giving points for development of voice both in writing and speaking, and points for facilitating the conversation, indicates to students that these are important processes that rely on listening carefully and not just speaking a lot.

■ With so many cross-cultural dynamics, it can be helpful to create a seating chart and then draw arrows from the speakers to the people they seem to be addressing. This may help you see some patterns that could be opening up or restricting access to the floor. For example, how often do students ask questions inviting responses from everyone? Are there a number of two-way conversations? If you do see patterns restricting the conversation, you could take a break or create a pause for reflection time.

■ It can be useful to have a round robin at the end of every seminar so that students can address microaggressions if they experienced any. The process of seminar cannot really be separated from its content, so encouraging students to speak about either can be liberating.

# Chapter 9

# Electronically Speaking

Online seminars offer new possibilities for faculty and students beyond the place-bound, face-to-face seminar. They allow participants to be anywhere they choose, and because the interaction is in writing, faculty can more easily assess each student's participation. At present, asynchronous discussions appear to be the norm. Because they are designed with questions posed by the faculty member, I do not categorize them as seminars. In these discussions students use a "writing voice." They use third person pronouns, state points rather than framing them as opinions, and rarely ask questions. Students have a great deal of time to respond, and this also allows multiple threads or topics to develop. Online seminars, on the other hand, are centered on students' questions, and held at an appointed time with everyone present. Responses are more spontaneous than in asynchronous discussions, and students need to respond quickly to ideas. In these, students use the "talking voice." They use first person pronouns, state opinions and personal experience, and ask questions (Campbell, 2003). In some ways, then, online seminars are similar to face-to-face ones because students raise their own questions and they come together at a particular time. For that reason, I will focus on online seminars in this chapter.

## DIFFERENCES BETWEEN WRITING AND SPEAKING

The most salient difference between the two types of seminars is the difference between speaking and writing. Writing creates a spatial organization of ideas rather than the temporal organization in face-to-face seminars. Consequently, writing changes the language students use in four ways that we need to consider if we choose this approach to seminars.

The first way that language is different online is that to take a turn in an online conversation, students write mostly in complete sentences. Sentences can be long and are marked with punctuation. These are spatial signals, not the auditory ones we use in conversations. We speak in short bursts that can be filled with false starts

(*The j- j- j- I mean jargon*) or other dysfluencies. Speakers don't always complete a sentence because in speaking we rely on verbal and nonverbal cues from our listeners. If our listeners are nodding or saying *uh huh* we assume they understand what we're saying. Other cues we notice are gestures, facial expressions, tone of voice, intonation, and body orientation such as when others turn towards or away from us. Students lose this information when the medium is online writing, so it is sometimes hard for them to know if anyone has understood a particular point.

The second way that online seminars are different is the increased planning time that students have when writing. Well-formed sentences are one indication of this planning. Another feature of planning is that it is possible for students to use word processing to create well-composed posts because they do not have to constantly monitor what everyone is doing; instead, they are looking at a screen with posts, a reduced field of information. Of course, there are times when students respond spontaneously and quickly to other students and it is clear that they are more focused on their ideas than their form. Still, these seminars are slow paced in comparison with face-to-face seminars because students need to read, think, sometimes reread, and then type. In addition, technical issues can slow down the process. I counted the words in two lively seminars, one online and the other face-to-face and in the latter students uttered nearly twice as many words as in the other. Of course, a major difference in the two seminars was the number of participants, with seven in the online seminar and sixteen in the face-to-face one.

The third way writing shapes language is that online seminars are stored and searchable, so students can refer back to their own posts or others' posts. In face-to-face seminars, on the other hand, one of the major negotiations is to reiterate or reformulate ideas so that everyone is clear about the ideas being contributed. We use phrases such as *that's not what I'm saying*. Our memories are not sufficient to recall everyone's exact words, so we get the gist of what others say and build on it or contrast it with our own ideas. Of course, neither writing nor speaking assures complete understanding. Students often reformulate what they mean in seminars and even then they may not be sure they are conveying their ideas clearly to others by saying, *what I think I mean is* or *did you get that?* In online writing, though, students can store and retrieve posts electronically, affording more access to everyone's ideas, but we cannot be sure of complete comprehension.

The fourth way that writing shapes language is that it makes access to everyone's ideas more possible; online seminars can be more inclusive. The student only needs to decide to post, so in theory, everyone's voice can be included. In face-to-face seminars, students may hear the conversation flow by them and be unable to jump in. Those who are more prepared or quicker at voicing their ideas can leave very little time for others who need more time to reflect or are shy. In online seminars students may still feel pressured because of time limitations, and they may hesitate to interrupt the flow of the conversation, but they can begin formulating a post at any time. There are different rules for timing a response based, not on nonverbal cues, but on typographical conventions. When they are sure about what they want to say, they simply push "enter."

For all of these reasons, online seminars are useful for students who may feel particular pressures in face-to-face settings, such as international or shy students. Students from the Far East or Southeast Asia, for example, often find it difficult to speak in face-to-face seminars. The cultural model of education in their countries is still teacher-centered, and they feel a pressure to be correct when they voice their contributions—correct in their ideas and correct in their English. One researcher teaching in New Zealand had a class that included some international Asian students. The New Zealanders noticed that in online discussions Asian students presented their ideas more consistently than in face-to-face situations. One New Zealander wrote, "[The online discussion] also gave boundaries to people like myself who talk too fast and too much." (Campbell, 2004, p.11). Although this study focused on asynchronous discussions, these points are applicable to online seminars because of the written format. Findings from other studies regarding Chinese and Southeast Asian students suggest that in face-to-face situations they may be hesitant to speak because they don't want to make a mistake and lose face, and they believe they may take too much time to formulate their ideas, thus wasting class time. In addition, they do not want to interrupt another speaker. From the students' point of view, if all students are participating in a synchronous seminar, they develop a sense of community. As an added benefit, nonnative speakers can gain confidence by noting flaws in the writing of native speakers.

## ONLINE DISCUSSIONS

What are some of the ways students create solidarity, perform identity, and deal with power in online conversations? Because I did not find any research on undergraduate online seminars, I decided to compare two types of online conversations—a discussion and eight seminars—to determine characteristics specific to online seminars. We will focus first on the online discussions. I analyzed transcriptions from a class of 57 students in a General Education course at a mid-sized eastern university. The faculty member divided the class into groups of seven or eight, posed five questions about a movie they had seen in class, and gave them a 45-minute time limit. Students didn't have a lot of time to compose their ideas, so their sentences were not always well formed and there were spelling errors in the transcriptions. Still, their conversations are coherent, even when there are interruptions.

## Creating Solidarity

In this discussion, students find ways to create solidarity by claiming common ground. In both cases this causes a divergence from the assignment. In (1) as students are agreeing about how they will move through the questions, Tim brings up a test they had taken, but Caroline immediately brings the group back to the questions. Note that in this and all subsequent transcriptions I do not correct what students wrote.

(1)

| | |
|---|---|
| *Tim*: | works for me . . . not to get off topic but am I the only one who thought that test we took last week kinda sucked? |
| *Elaine*: | it was really hard I dont think I did well at all |
| *Caroline*: | definitely harder than the first one |
| *Levi*: | yes it was really hard if we compare it to the first one |
| *Peter*: | yeah it was . . . there wasnt much on there that was in the notes |
| *Caroline*: | so next question? |

The words Tim uses to introduce his comments on the test, *not to get off topic but*, is an alert to everyone that he will go off topic. This is common in face-to-face seminars as well (*not to be sexist*, *but* or *not to be a goody two-shoes*, *but*). Why does Tim complain about the text when he knows that the faculty member will read his words? Part of the reason is no doubt the online forum—a chat room is usually informal and there is no authority present; part of the reason is that he performs an identity as a student complaining about the work load. Complaining is a common activity students engage in outside of class. His comment also diverges from the assignment, which is to answer five questions. In research on face-to-face classroom discussions, researchers have found that students diverging from the assigned task may be testing the power relations in the group to find out what may or may not be said. This sort of comment can be useful to challenge what is going on (Bergvall & Remlinger, 1996). In this case, Tim introduces his comment as others are coming online, so it can be seen as small talk rather than a direct challenge, and Caroline's redirecting of the conversation, "so next question?" focuses the discussion with no more attention to Tim's comment.

In another group, two students also diverge from the task when they reveal that they know each other from high school. As in (1), they are also engaged in small talk as they wait for others to join (2):

(2)

| | |
|---|---|
| *Seth*: | wait you went to fhs right |
| *Shanice*: | yes! Omg I knew you did |
| *Seth*: | ha-ha |

*Seth:*  I was going to say i've deff seen you in class and was like im pretty sure she went to fhs

*Shanice:*  haha yupp

*Seth:*  love how we are supposed to be discussing movie questions and it turns into a highschool reuion haha

Since neither of these students had seen the movie, they could not answer the questions. Perhaps because they were assigned to interact online in a chat forum, they made a personal connection, reinforcing their identities as experiencing the same high school. Seth also reveals that he had thought to himself that he knew her, "[I] was like I'm pretty sure she went to fhs," using reported speech, a common feature of face-to-face conversation. Reported speech is used to recreate a situation quoting oneself or someone else in a creative, lively way. In online discussions and seminars, I only noticed it in this instance.

Of the 57 students, 16 who took part in the chats stated they had not seen the movie, like Seth and Shanice. Although students do come unprepared to face-to-face seminars, they do not usually admit voluntarily to not having read the text. The relative anonymity of electronic forums may encourage this honesty, but it is surprising since the faculty member stated that he would read the chat logs. Some researchers have addressed this issue. They find that when people are online, they focus more on the computer screen than the audience. This depersonalizes the discussion leading people to reveal more about themselves and to be less polite than if they were face to face with others (Johnstone, 2002). Being separated from other students helps create anonymity.

The students were unfamiliar with using the chat medium for discussion in this face-to-face class, and in some cases they borrowed from other online media. In (3) Amber seems quite pleased that another student agrees with her point. She borrows from texting conventions with her comments and *lol* in the last two lines.

(3)

*Amber:*  and last question answer, I think I feel less favorable about the way laws are made in congress and would though the process works it needs to evolve into the 21st century

*Amber:*  things that could be done to improve it woudl be such a small issue asn one person speaks at a time, and nothing is really happens behind closed doors.

*Jenna:*  I agree with you there too. You're totally right

*Amber:*  ahhh ya made me bluxh

*Amber:*  blush

*Amber:*  lol

**141**

In a face-to-face seminar Amber might have blushed, but it is more likely that here she is just expressing pleasure for having a good idea. Jenna gives Amber an emphatic agreement, "I agree with you there too. You're totally right." This is a way of giving face to Amber and creating solidarity. In this chat session, students used the word "agree" much more often than in face-to-face seminars, where using that verb is quite rare. I counted the word 30 times. In addition, I found "true" and "exactly" used often. Although agreement is usually a sign of creating common ground, except in (3), most agreement is rather perfunctory.

## Face

Unlike face-to-face seminars where disagreement is common, I found only one case of a disagreement in (4):

(4)

Gary: I think thw whole law making process itself is very counterproductive and needs to be changed if we want to see the results needed to fix our nation as a whole

Jorge: I don't think the process is counterproductive but more the increasing polorization in congress prevents it from being productive

Christa: I think May way back the system worked but now it's just a waste of time and too much back and forth to get something passed

Christa: *maybe

Gary: whether it is the process as a whole or the polarization, it still needs to be changed in order to actually accomplish things

Gary begins by calling the legislative process counterproductive and Jorge disagrees, claiming that it is polarization that is the problem. In his last post, Gary accepts both possibilities and calls for change, softening the disagreement that Jorge raised so that there was no face threat to Jorge. A face threat would have been a direct challenge to Jorge's positive self-image. By avoiding it, Gary underscores the importance of common ground or solidarity in the conversation. The fact that there was only this one disagreement could be due to lack of time to delve into each question, or that students had to rely on their memory of that event. In addition, in viewing the movie, they may not have arrived at a complex understanding of the issues being raised. This online discussion provides an excellent way for the faculty member to assess each student's response to the movie, and the conversation has some elements in common with online seminars.

## ONLINE SEMINARS

In order to analyze online seminars, I turned to my colleague, José Gómez, who has been fine-tuning online seminars for the past 15 years. He found a way to incorporate them into his online summer classes despite the dearth of information about using seminars in such courses. Gómez regularly teaches two online courses. Each is organized with two weekly themes set up as legal questions requiring a yes or no response. In a recent course called Crime and Punishment, he asked "Should the 'insanity defense' be abolished?" and "Have police brutality and excessive force become severe problems in need of special solutions?" For each theme, instead of lectures, students are assigned online readings and they also hear debates on these themes from public broadcasting. Gómez organizes the students into groups of eight that work together all quarter. At least one day before the seminar, each student addresses the theme in a "critical comment" of 250–300 words, posted on an asynchronous discussion board. After the deadline for critical comments, students each post four responses to the critical comments. These responses must be substantive, explaining why they agree or disagree, providing more information, or expanding on the comment.

All of this work is in preparation for the culminating activity, the online seminar. At least one hour before it begins, students each post an open-ended question on the theme. A student facilitator is responsible for reviewing the questions and guiding the conversation and this responsibility rotates through the group. Gómez uses student facilitators because he believes students will express themselves more freely when the faculty member is not present. Nonetheless, he sometimes makes his presence known if he believes it is necessary. At the end of the seminar, each student posts final comments on the theme. At no time are students required to take a position on the legal questions. Instead, the emphasis is on analysis and critical thinking.

Gómez reports that online seminars are the most important element in his course. Students feel that when they are interacting in real time, they create a dynamic community and have the opportunity to synthesize their learning. He builds community in other ways as well. He encourages students to post a personal profile on the discussion board, and requires a passport-type photo rather than a more artistic one.

### Agreeing

I analyzed eight seminars from Gómez's class. Each lasted two hours and an average of seven students participated. A common element in these online seminars, which I also noted in the online discussion, was the use of *I agree*. I counted 56 instances, with 11 in the seminar with the most complex conversation —the highest number of any seminar. Like the chat sessions, there were time

**143**

constraints, and the use of *I agree* may have helped students making a contribution understand quickly that their points were accepted. After all, there are no head nods or *uh huhs* in online communication. In about one third of the cases, students agreed specifically with a named student, and at times this seemed necessary because they did not always post immediately after the statement that they agreed with. In reviewing the types of comments students made after agreeing, I believe that some students agreed simply to maintain a presence in the seminar. Quite often inactive students do not develop an idea further.

## Getting the Floor

Getting the floor can be problematic in online seminars. Many researchers seem to think that students can get the floor merely by composing their messages and sending them. Gómez asks his students to follow a rule: to use ellipses to indicate when they wish to have the floor. In most cases, once they have posted this signal, they can begin their post. If more than one student wants the floor, the facilitator gives the order of comments. Gómez also requires that students write their posts in short phrases using ellipses if they have not finished or a period if they have. This allows others to read posts more quickly. In face-to-face communication, students do not get the floor unless others in the group acknowledge their comment in some way. Head nods or eye contact can be enough to know that others are listening. In electronic seminars, unless someone comments on a post, a student will not gain the floor. Gómez has seen students write, *please respond!*

Unlike face-to-face seminars, in both the online discussion about the film and the seminars that I analyzed, students worked on answering each question that was posed and checked with each other before moving on. In face-to-face seminars this does not happen often, most likely because rather than seven to eight people, there are 25 or more. Questions and ideas can sometimes remain un-resolved because the conversation moves on. In online seminars there are fewer cues for gauging reactions. I noted that many students use *true* or *very true* as a possible replacement for *uh huh*.

## A Focus on Dialogue

At the end of both the online chat and seminars, students thanked the facilitator or each other, or wrote a compliment, such as *nice working with you* or *see you next Thursday*. These leave-takings are not found in face-to-face seminars where this usually occurs after class. The written record for these online seminars, though, contained many politeness formulas. Overall these seminars appeared more courteous because of these features of agreement and formal leave-taking. Gómez believes that part of the reason for this courtesy has to do with a distinction he makes between debate and dialogue; he insists that students use dialogue. He provides students with a handout adapted from Berman (1993) and expanded, as shown in Box 9.1.

In past years when students did not have this information, Gómez reports that students were often uncivil. This may be due to inexperience with seminars and confusion about the goals of collaborative learning. Students may also have drawn on norms in online forums where the conversation is often uncivil. Once students understand the overarching goals of seminar are collaborative learning and developing a voice, and they have some information about techniques to use, Gómez reports that they have productive conversations.

## Cross-Cultural Dynamics

One feature of online seminars that researchers applaud is the reduction of cues about social identities. They claim that online discussions are more egalitarian and students of different genders and ethnicities participate more. In a study comparing online and face-to-face discussions in each of three classes at a large southwestern university, Joanna Wolfe (2000) tested this claim. She found that white males participated the most in face-to-face discussions, Hispanic women participated within the mean, and white women and Hispanic men participated below the mean. In online discussions, white women increased their participation by 50% but Hispanic women decreased their participation. Participation by Hispanic and white males was near the mean, indicating an increase in talk among Hispanic males and a decrease among white males. This suggests that white women and Hispanic men may participate more in online discussions, but we have no evidence for online seminars as yet. We also do not have research on the differences in participation among other minoritized groups.

## Performing Identity

Indeed, many features of identity are masked in online written communication. Writing disguises regional or foreign accents, the sound of a voice, tone, intonation, and the nonverbal actions each of us perform as we speak. Skin color, clothing, and adornment are also missing. Names can sometimes indicate gender or ethnicity, but not always. Using written language in seminars can reduce information we routinely notice in face-to-face conversations. This can create a greater equality in pursuing ideas and collaboration, but it can possibly undermine creating a community of learners. That is, to create a community, we need to know each other, and part of knowing others is to know about social identities. There is reason to believe, then, that students perform identity there is a lack of information. In the online discussions I analyzed, a student performed the identity of student by complaining about a test; in addition, two students realized they were from the same high school.

# BOX 9.1 COMPARISON OF DIALOGUE AND DEBATE

| Dialogue | Debate |
|---|---|
| Dialogue is collaborative. Two or more sides work together toward common understanding. | Debate is oppositional. Two sides oppose each other and attempt to prove each other wrong. |
| In dialogue, finding common ground is the goal. | In debate, winning is the goal. |
| In dialogue, one listens to the other side(s) in order to understand, find meaning, and find agreement. | In debate, one listens to the other side in order to find flaws and to counter its arguments. |
| Dialogue enlarges and possibly changes a participant's point of view. | Debate affirms a person's own point of view. |
| Dialogue complicates positions and issues. | Debate simplifies positions and issues. |
| Dialogue reveals assumptions for re-evaluation. | Debate defends assumptions as truth. |
| Dialogue causes introspection on one's own position. | Debate causes critique of the other position. |
| It is acceptable to change one's position. | It is a sign of weakness and defeat to change one's position. |
| Dialogue is flexible in nature. | Debate is rigid in nature. |
| Dialogue stresses the skill of synthesis. | Debate stresses the skill of analysis. |
| Dialogue opens the possibility of reaching a better solution than any of the original solutions. | Debate defends one's own position as the best solution and excludes other solutions. |
| Dialogue strives for multiplicity in perspective. | Debate strives for singularity in perspective. |
| Dialogue affirms the relationship between the participants through collaboration. | Debate affirms one's own strength in opposition to other points of view. |
| Dialogue creates an open-minded attitude, an openness to change. | Debate creates a close-minded attitude, a determination to be right. |

| Dialogue | Debate |
| --- | --- |
| In dialogue, one submits one's best thinking, knowing that other peoples' reflections will help improve it rather than destroy it. | In debate, one submits one's best thinking and defends it against challenges to show that it is right. |
| Dialogue calls for temporarily suspending one's beliefs. | Debate calls for investing wholeheartedly in one's beliefs. |
| In dialogue, one searches for basic agreements. | In debate, one searches for glaring differences. |
| In dialogue, one searches for strengths in the other position. | In debate one searches for flaws and weaknesses in the other position. |
| Dialogue involves a real concern for the other person and seeks to not alienate or offend. | Debate involves a countering of the other position without focusing on feelings or relationship, and often belittles or deprecates the other position. |
| Dialogue assumes that many people have pieces of the answer, and that together they can put them into a workable answer. | Debate assumes there is a right answer and that someone has it. |
| Dialogue encourages de-polarization of an issue. | Debate encourages polarization of an issue. |
| In dialogue, everyone is part of the solution to the problem. | In debate, one person or viewpoint wins over the other. |
| Dialogue affirms the idea of people learning from each other. | Debate affirms the idea of people learning individually in competition with others. |
| Dialogue remains open-ended. | Debate implies a conclusion. |

To test whether or not students disclosed their social identities in online seminars, I analyzed those in my colleague's class for markers of identity. I found many instances of students marking their identities. In one case, the facilitator asked, "Is anybody else a parent?" Of the seven students, four were. Since everyone responded and no one questioned why they were being asked to identify as parent or non-parent, it is clear that the group felt that knowing more about each other's identity would help them understand each other's perspectives. Most often, however, students self-identify rather than asking others to do so. They provide information about their activities which can indicate age and social groups, and high school experiences I give three examples in (5), each chosen from different seminars:

(5)

*Chad*: Once again, I am 36 and I remember the president being shot. Now Hinkley is out there on the streets walking where my children play. That to me seems insane!

*Renee*: He was smart enough to make it into college and being crazy.

*Bianca*: Smart enough has nothing to do with it. I am schizophrenic and bipolar. I take 12 medications. I am about to receive my Bachelor's degree.

*Jordan*: If they are committing these types of crimes at that age then I think it has to do with their environment and also their age (again, not an expert).

Each student gives specific information: "I am 36," "my children," "I am schizophrenic and bipolar," "not an expert." These are all ways of introducing social identity into the conversation to indicate either their authority to comment or to hedge that authority. Another researcher found the same phenomenon in online discussions. In one case, a student even announced the birth of her child the day she delivered it (Cox & Cox, 2008). As I was analyzing these seminars, I could not stop myself from noticing who used poor grammar or made spelling mistakes, how often students contributed, and the quality of their comments. I believe that because I had so few cues about their identities, I was searching for ways to create them. I noticed in one seminar that the facilitator was also the student making the most comments. She gained power by writing so often, but she also gained power through her authority as a well-prepared student critiquing ideas and offering new ones.

## Showing Solidarity

Besides indicating identity, students also showed solidarity in these online seminars, as part of facework. Face is the positive public image we have of ourselves and facework is the ritual we engage in for any conversation to take place. For example, students support each other by praising ideas, giving compliments, and agreeing before disagreeing. These are all ways to maintain the face of other students and to assure that they themselves have maintained face. (See Chapter 7.) In these online seminars they often assure others that their idea is useful: *that's a great point* or *that's a really good idea*. These compliments give face to other students and are courteous. In (6) we see another way of complimenting in a seminar about police interrogation:

(6)
*Paula*: At first I started to focus on the cons on videotaping interrogations like the point brought up about the possibility of a person shutting up and not cooperating when being videotaped. but then I believe Jasmine brought a different perspective to light for me

Bringing a perspective to light is a metaphor that we often use: light clarifies an idea and when we see the light, we understand something new. Paula acknowledges another student's point about a subject not cooperating, and then names Jasmine for bringing up an especially important point from her point of view. Jasmine thanks Paula (not shown here), recognizing the compliment. Paula and Jasmine have gained face in this post and they collaboratively deepened the conversation.

## Facework

Students also use facework to make sure others feel valued as part of the group. In (7) the facilitator, Denise, has posted Miles' question for the next point of discussion, and then asks if he wants to add anything:

(7)
*Miles*: Well I'm guilty of not reading the questions before posting this so it seems somewhat similar to Shelley's but I was just thinking [. . .]
*Denise*: I did the same myself Miles, but I think your question brings up a really valid point.

In this case, Miles' confession (*Well I'm guilty*) may have come as a result of Denise's questioning if he wanted to add anything after writing his question for the group. He may have seen her question as a face threat because his question was so similar to another one they already addressed. This seems to be how Denise interprets Miles' response because she admits to the same mistake, and then adds that his question is valid. Her expression of solidarity, "a really valid point," and common ground, "I did the same," is not necessary to the inquiry, but it does acknowledge Miles' question and his actions as acceptable. Students then discuss his question, also treating it as valid. In this way, Denise and the group made sure that Miles did not lose face.

In disagreeing, students also use facework. In (8), Aron questions Julie, who clearly takes offense, and after some negotiation, the facilitator, Tony, suggests moving on:

(8)

Aron: so you are saying that, that group of college kids who decide to streak are future offenders?

Julie: no      dont put words in my mouth. If someone exposes themselves to a child or other adult for sexual pleasure.

Aron: I wasnt trying to put words in your mouth i was trying to better understand.

Julie: sorry

Aron: your views. sorry.

Julie: i misinterrupted tone. my fault.

Tony: Ok, maybe we should ask another question.

Julie: my emotions are running pretty high right now.

Aron: no worries

In this exchange, Aron uses the phrase "so you are saying" when there is no indication of Julie writing that streakers are future offenders. By beginning his comment with *so*, he seems to be using it as a synonym for "therefore," but *so* can also introduce a new topic: *So, on another topic.* It is ambiguous. Julie clearly understands the "so" to mean therefore and says, "don't put words in my mouth." This is a reprimand with no softeners and it threatens Aron's face. They both write "sorry" with Julie adding that it was her fault and that her emotions are running high. Resolving this face threat takes very little time, but obviously one of the problems is that Julie had difficulty understanding Aron's tone: "i misinterrupted [misinterpreted] tone. my fault." He might have chosen a better way to phrase his question by omitting "you're saying." Several other students introduce complications they want to address by prefacing their paraphrase with *so you're saying* in this seminar. One implication is that wording is important especially without other cues such as tone of voice and facial gestures. Another point to consider is that Julie may have responded harshly to Aron, but their apologies are not equal. Both say they are sorry, but she adds that it is her fault, and then she adds two reasons: that she misinterpreted his tone, and her emotions were running high. Aron, for his part, does not offer more than the simple "sorry" for his words. Researchers have found that women are generally more polite in online communications than men (Herring, 2003).

In a study that examined disagreements in asynchronous discussions (Lapadat, 2007, p.89), some of the same patterns of prefacing a disagreement with agreement occur as in face-to-face seminars (Chapter 7). In this graduate class, Patrick, who teaches adults, writes that teachers should not have to tolerate deviant behavior and that they do not have time to individualize instruction for individual students. Elaine, who teaches special education classes responds in (9), prefacing her disagreement with two sentences to acknowledging Patrick's point as a common struggle for all teachers. Then she disagrees.

(9)

*Elaine*: I appreciated your comments particularly about classroom management and the real possibility of latching on to a bottle of asprin.
Deviant behavior in classrooms is something we all struggle with. I
think many of the ideas in this article such as students being able to
make connections to prior learning to gain understanding, and the
importance of ensuring that students do have the necessary background
knowledge so that connections can be made are important points for
us as teachers [. . .] In order to provide educational opportunities for
all students we must not only recognize what their needs are but have
the necessary resources to address those needs, whether that be in the
form of trained personnel or materials. Maybe then we wouldn't need
to clutch the bottle of asprin? What do you think?

Elaine's disagreement begins with the third sentence, *I think* and she points out
that the article under discussion provides a counterpoint to Patrick's argument.
She then argues that all teachers need necessary resources in their classrooms.
She saves face for Patrick by keeping her disagreement impersonal. She focuses
on the author's argument and then she invites Patrick's response, "what do you
think?" Besides reinforcing her identity as a teacher who, like Patrick, has
problems with classroom management, she also creates authority by referring to
the text. She indirectly points out that he is responding from his own practice
rather than integrating his prior experience with the theories presented in the
text. Elaine's contribution thus deepens the discussion by suggesting a way that
experience and theory can be linked, and by focusing closely on the author's
argument.

## Claiming Authority

As a graduate student, Elaine may be comfortable creating authority for herself
in seminar. Undergraduate students often hedge their authority in a number of
ways. Benwell and Stokoe (2002) suggest that disclaimers such as *I don't know*
or *not an expert* likely serve multiple functions. They can, for example, point to
the student's academic identity as a novice and act as a hedge for not having
experience with the topic. As we saw in Chapter 7, disclaimers can also function
as a preface to a disagreement and indicate that the student does not accept the
argument presented by someone else. In one seminar I analyzed, the conversation
around the question "Should the 'insanity defense' be abolished?" moved to
funding programs for the mentally ill. Monica suggests a solution using a possible
hedge in (10):

(10)

*Monica*: Couldn't positive programs bring in an income? Or more fines and fees before incarceration? Just a thought.

The hedge "just a thought" seems to indicate that Monica is not invested in her idea. It is "just" a thought. Three students point out problems with this idea because many people can't pay. Monica turns out to be invested in her idea after all, because she persists with it in (11):

(11)

*Monica*: I think the struggles of having to pay a fine are much more reasonable than the troubles caused from being incarcerated. Thank goodness for payment options!

Monica may be using the phrase, "just a thought," as an invitation for others to comment because she uses it once again, later in the seminar. In this case, then, the phrase does not function as a hedge. It is often the case that words and phrases have more than one meaning, and we are often trying to understand which one the speaker is using, as in the disagreement in (8). In this case, Monica's comments in this seminar are reactions to the ideas of others, and she does not seem to reflect on the implications of her ideas. Others, though, are quick to do that.

Using a hedge disclaiming authority for an idea is very rare in these online seminars. In face-to-face seminars, however, hedges are quite common. Students use many hedges including *maybe*, *probably*, *it seems*, *kind of*, and *in a way*. More research will be needed to understand why this difference exists, but one reason could be that although online seminars are more conversational than online discussions, they are still far less spontaneous than face-to-face conversations. Students have the time to formulate their ideas before writing them and they may be more focused on producing a good argument than hedging their own authority. The stated goal of seminars in Gómez's class is to create a personal synthesis and I find students considering each other's comments carefully before moving to their own ideas. As time goes by in the term, they probably also realize the importance of phrasing their ideas well because they can review their contributions to past seminars.

## ASSESSMENT

Researchers have been interested in evaluating the collaborative learning that may be occurring in online posts by examining login times, types of responses, and to whom students responded (e.g., Wise, Perera, Hsiao, Speer, & Marbouti, 2012). Clearly, asking good questions and contributing ideas that deepen the conversation are important to note. It might also be useful to realize that students will probably not be consistent in every post every week across the academic term. In my experience with face-to-face seminars, I find that the text, questions, and conversation may be more or less absorbing to them, and, in addition, they have time constraints such as family, work schedules, and personal concerns that may intervene. None of us is completely consistent in the ways we interact with others. Certainly there are a few students who attend every seminar, come well prepared, respond appropriately to other students, and help to deepen the conversation, but it is rare to have a student who is always "on." And, if there are students who are always "on," then others may allow themselves to coast. Instead, it is more likely that students will be more motivated for some seminars than others, and that their participation will reflect their interest, preparedness, and knowledge. Just as important as noting students' consistency in seminar is tracing their development in understanding the concepts and principles introduced in the reading and seminars over the term. When they begin referring to the readings and naming theories or approaches to questions, they gain authority for their ideas and develop a critical voice. Online seminars are clearly a good choice for helping students do this.

## CONCLUSION

As technology changes and becomes less expensive, a wider variety of online seminars will be possible. Some platforms already allow students to indicate they want to speak using a mic. The facilitator calls on that person to actually voice their idea. Similarly, video conferencing may become more widely available. Mixing writing and speaking offers some advantages. For students who do not type quickly or accurately, speaking would offer quicker access to the conversation. As I have pointed out in this chapter, writing provides the seminar group with a written record, which is useful for reviewing ideas and assessing them. Researchers will need to assess these changes as they become more available in the undergraduate curriculum.

## BEST PRACTICES

- Facilitators can model building on ideas, asking questions for clarification or to delve deeper into a topic, and making connections to the texts. By telling students that you are modeling the sort of authority you want them to imitate, students may focus more on their authority than your assessments. Using an informal, talking voice can encourage students as well because the faculty member's authority as an expert is already established.

- Asking students to select a facilitator or assigning one each time creates a collaborative atmosphere and helps students develop skills in monitoring what is

**153**

going on. In the online seminars I examined, facilitators asked other students if they had anything to add if they had not posted on a question. All but one skillfully made transitions between the conversation and the next question they needed to discuss by writing, for example, "I think that leads nicely into your own question." Facilitators can also examine the ways they were able to direct the conversation as part of their self-assessment.

■ Providing clear guidelines for online seminars is essential. The most important guideline is that seminars must be linked to readings. For online seminars, asking students to post a question on the reading that they want to discuss prior to the conversation helps students prepare for the conversation. They should receive guidelines about the platform they are using, the number of posts that are expected, and conventions they should use. In the online seminar at my college, José Gómez provided a list of possible abbreviations and asked students to limit themselves to those. He also stipulated that after posting, students should type ellipses to indicate they had something to add. Another important directive was that they should post in short phrases followed by ellipses so that others could read more efficiently. Waiting for students to write and post long responses takes up valuable seminar time because many students type and read slowly.

■ Online seminars should have clear time limits and guidelines. The guidelines should include who will facilitate, how students should interact in a civil manner, and the goals. My colleague posed a theme for each seminar and assigned students to post their questions one hour prior to seminar. This format allowed each student to explore an area of their choosing and everyone could prepare for seminar knowing most of the questions.

■ One of the keys to effective online seminars according to my colleague is to ask students to prepare a final statement which is a response to the seminar theme. This allows students to write a synthesis of what they have learned and it is useful for assessing the development of their thinking.

■ According to Cain (2012), research indicates that brainstorming is very effective when done online and it can help participants feel a sense of community. It may be useful to include at least one brainstorming activity during the term as a way of working on synthesis of the material.

■ To assess online seminars, you can use the rubric from the Best Practices section of Chapter 2. In addition, Lalli and Feger (2005) have developed a rubric for mathematics, which can be adapted to other disciplines.

# Glossary

**Academic English:** A way of speaking that uses terminology from academic disciplines as well as drawing on the grammar of Standard English. It is a register in linguistic terms and it is used in speaking and writing.

**Accent:** A way of pronouncing words or phrases. Everyone has an accent because we all have particular ways of pronouncing words and using intonation in our varieties of English (or any other language). Linguists see pronunciation and intonation as part of dialects and styles.

**Agency:** Having the power or capacity to act. In seminar this means having a voice in the conversation.

**Arguing to persuade:** An argument used in academic discourse, both spoken and written, which states a claim and provides evidence from well documented sources. The point is to persuade.

**Arguing to win:** An argument used mostly in everyday conversation, which states a claim with evidence that usually from personal opinion, personal experience, or hearsay. The point is to win.

**Brainstorming:** Students generate lists of ideas. The goal is to make a long list and to be inventive. No judgment or criticism is permitted. Building on others' ideas is useful.

**Code-switch:** Changing from one style to another, one dialect to another, or one language to another. It is a common phenomenon.

**Community of practice:** Lave and Wenger (1991), who coined this phrase discuss "legitimate peripheral participation" as a crucial part of any learning. Learning is a social experience similar to an apprenticeship. The apprentice participates in a particular practice and also observes. They reject the notion that learning is a purely cognitive experience.

**Conversational moves:** We are always doing something with our words. In seminars, for example, we ask or answer a question, agree or disagree, clarify or ask for clarification, apologize, invite responses, and compliment.

**Creaky voice:** A style of speaking that women currently use more than men possibly to signal authority. It is also called vocal fry. One way to produce it is to pronounce the word "button" without pronouncing the "t." The raspy sound you produce instead of the "t" can be prolonged.

**Cultural models:** These are simplified theories or stories that we use to quickly understand and make sense of the world. We have an idea of "vacation" of "classroom" of "running for office" and each of these is a cultural model based on our socialization. We can have these models even if we never engage in a particular activity because they are part of our culture. Examining them reveals the patterns that create the model.

**Dialect:** A dialect is a variety of a language with a complete set of grammatical rules, vocabulary or lexicon, and way of pronouncing words. It is the same as a language, then, except that its speakers do not hold political and social power. Some dialects may not have a written grammar and dictionary and literature.

**Face:** The positive value each person holds of their public persona. We negotiate our face and others' faces in each conversation. Our face can change according to the situation, other speakers, and goals.

**Face threat:** We can threaten someone's face by being direct as in giving a command or order or being impolite. The context, which includes the situation, place, who can overhear, the relationship between the speakers, and their status all play a role in determining whether or not someone's words constitute a face threat to another person. Face threats usually cause a problem such as loss of face.

**Facework:** The activities we use in conversation to maintain enough harmony to complete them. We need to show common ground and courtesy to others so that they maintain our face as well as theirs.

**Gender binary:** The ideology that there are only two genders, male and female. It leaves out transgendered people as well as others who question their gender in various ways.

**Hedge:** Words and phrases that mitigate or soften the force of a statement. *Possibly, maybe, it seems, sort of,* and *in some ways* are all hedges that are widely used. Hedges can soften a disagreement, express uncertainty, or indicate that the next word is not the exact one.

**Heteronormativity:** An ideology that heterosexuality is the norm and should be the norm. We call up this ideology by referring to gender as being composed of just two types, male and female.

**High-Considerateness Style:** A style speakers use that allows about a half a second or more between turns.

**High-Involvement Style:** In this style, speakers often overlap in order to show rapport or solidarity, they use machine-gun questioning, and they find pauses uncomfortable.

**Identity:** I use the term "social identities" to refer to the many factors that influence the way we talk, move, dress, behave, and the values we hold. These factors include gender, race, ethnicity, class, education, age, sexual orientation, nationality, geographic region, religion, etc. In conversations we produce social identities. They are not fixed and stable features; in addition, we can position others and they can position us to focus on just one of these identities.

**Ideology:** The often unspoken beliefs that seem commonplace and that order our social worlds.

**LGBTQ:** This abbreviation usually refers to a community of lesbian, gay, bisexual, transsexual, queer, and questioning people. Those who are questioning are not yet sure of their identity in this community.

**Linguistic repertoire:** Ways of talking including dialects, registers, styles, lexicon, borrowed phrases, and phrases to maintain face. It also includes all of the intonation patterns, tones of voice, voice quality (breathiness, creaky voice), and other musical features of language including timing in conversations.

**Mainstream English:** The English of the government, schools, and written news media. It is close to Standard English, but includes informal as well as formal English practices.

**Marginalization:** Students can feel intimidated by other students in the seminar and so they either do not participate at all or only participate minimally. Their voices, then, are pushed to the margins of the conversation instead of being heard and carefully considered.

**Microaggression:** The subtle slights and insults that privileged speakers may not be aware of. Privileged speakers are those who are not in a minoritized group and they often do not realize that they have privilege and power.

**Minoritized groups:** Social groups that are devalued. Traditionally these groups have been called "minorities" but "minoritized" captures the dynamics that are always present in social interactions and signals that a group's status is not always related to how many people are in it.

**Positioning:** Placing someone or ourselves in a particular social category in a conversation. This can be done with words or by ignoring someone, positioning them as an outsider.

**Power in conversation:** Having power in conversation means having agency—you can express your ideas. Other moves we associate with power are dominating the conversation either by controlling the floor or talking a lot. Students can also gain power by making controversial statements, using debate techniques, arguing to win, or using derisive tones that silence others. Taking a stance of authority, using academic discourse, and articulating new ideas are all ways of gaining power as well. Power shifts in conversations, and it must be granted to speakers by others.

**Register:** A set of terms and phrases that we learn at work, in college, and through the media. Softball players, government workers, hair dressers, and engineers all have particular terms they use. Many people are familiar with the register of a barista, for example, when they order coffee successfully at a specialized coffee shop. Academic English is a register. All disciplines have registers.

**Reported speech:** We interject what someone else said or might have said or thought into our own utterance. This can be a direct quote and it can be in the voice of that other person so that we are mimicking that person. Students introduce these quotes using *she said, she's like, she goes, she's all*. We can also report ideas that we had prior to the current conversation (*I was thinking at the time, what does that mean?*). Reported speech is useful to interject spontaneity, humor, or the flavor of another conversation. In seminars, it is mostly used to be indirect.

**Stance:** A speaker's attitude, belief, or assessment of what they are saying. In English we do not have to indicate a stance, but some ways that we do are *I think, I guess, I heard, the author writes*. A stance can provide a speaker with authority in seminar.

**Standard English.** The English that is taught in textbooks but that no one actually uses all of the time. The grammar rules, lexicon, and pronunciation are codified in grammar books and dictionaries and these do not change very rapidly, unlike the grammar and lexicon and pronunciation of mainstream English. It is primarily used in writing.

**Transition moments:** These are moments for a listener to take a turn. These occur when a speaker may invite a response from another by using their name or addressing a comment directly to them; or the other speaker may take a turn when the first speaker completes a sentence or clause, a phrase, or a word, or uses intonation in a way to indicate a complete thought.

**Vocal fry.** Also called creaky voice, it is a phenomenon of lowering the voice by vibrating the vocal chords at one end. One way to produce it is to pronounce "button" without pronouncing the "t." The raspy sound you produce instead of the "t" can be prolonged.

# References

Alim, H. S., & Baugh, J. (2007). *Talkin black talk: Language, education, and social change*. New York, NY & London: Teachers College Press.

Basturkmen, H. (1999). "Discourse in MBA seminars: Towards a description for pedagogical purposes." *English for Specific Purposes*, *18*, 63–80. doi:10.1016/S0889–4906(97)00049–5

Baumgarten, N., & House, J. (2010). "I think and I don't know in English as lingua franca and native English discourse." *Journal of Pragmatics*, *42*, 1184–1200.

Benwell, B. (2012). "Common-sense anti-racism in book group talk: The role of reported speech." *Discourse & Society*, *23*, 359–376.

Benwell, B., & Stokoe, E. H. (2002). "Constructing discussion tasks in university tutorials: shifting dynamics and identities." *Discourse Studies*, *4*, 429–453.

Bergvall, V. L., & Remlinger, K. A. (1996). "Reproduction, resistance and gender in educational discourse: The role of critical discourse analysis." *Discourse & Society*, *7*, 453–479.

Berman, S. (1993). "Comparison of dialogue and debate." *Focus on Study Circles: The Newsletter of the Study Circles Resource Center*. http://ipsdweb.ipsd.org/uploads/PDAC/ComparisonofDialogueandDebate_0310.pdf

Blackburn, M. V., & Clark, C. T. (2011). "Analyzing talk in a long-term literature discussion group: Ways of operating within LGBT-inclusive and queer discourses." *Reading Research Quarterly*, *46*, 222–248.

Bligh, D. A. (2000). *What's the use of lectures?* San Francisco, CA: Jossey-Bass.

Bonilla-Silva, E. (2002). "The linguistics of color blind racism: How to talk nasty about blacks without sounding racist." *Critical Sociology*, *28*, 41–64.

Bourdieu, P. (1991). *Language and symbolic power*. J. B. Thompson (Ed.) (Trans. G. Raymond & M. Adamson). Cambridge, MA: Harvard University Press.

Boysen, G. A., Vogel, D. L., Cope, M. A., & Hubbard, A. (2009). "Incidents of bias in college classrooms: Instructor and student perceptions." *Journal of Diversity in Higher Education*, *2*, 219–231. doi: 10.1037/a0017538

Bruffee, K. A. (1999). *Collaborative learning*. Baltimore, MD: Johns Hopkins University Press.

Buttny, R. (1997). "Reported speech in talking race on campus." *Human Communications Research, 23,* 477–506.

Cain, S. (2012). *Quiet: The power of introverts in a world that can't stop talking*. New York, NY: Crown.

Campbell, N. (2004). "Online discussion: A new tool for classroom integration?" *Communication Journal of New Zealand, 5,* 7–26.

Campbell, S. W. (2003). "Listening to the voices in an online class." *Qualitative Research Reports in Communication, 4,* 9–15.

Collins, P. H. (1993). "Toward a new vision: Race, class, and gender as categories of analysis and connection." *Race, Sex, and Class, 1,* 25–46.

Condon, W. (1976). "An analysis of behavioral organization." *Sign Language Studies, 13,* 285–318.

Condon, W., & Ogston, W. (1971). "Speech and body motion synchrony of the speaker-hearer." In D. Horton & J. Jenkins (Eds.). *The Perception of Language* (pp. 150–184). Columbus, OH: Charles E. Merrill.

Couper-Kuhlen, E. (1993). *English speech rhythm: Form and function in every-day verbal interaction*. Amsterdam & Philadelphia, PA: John Benjamins.

Cox, B., & Cox, B. (2008). "Developing interpersonal and group dynamics through asynchronous threaded discussions: The use of discussion board in collaborative learning." *Education, 128,* 553–565.

Eckert, P., & McConnell-Ginet, S. (2003). *Language and gender*. Cambridge: Cambridge University Press.

Elbow, P. (1986). *Embracing contraries: Explorations in learning and teaching*. New York, NY: Oxford University Press.

Erickson, F., & Shultz, J. (1982). *The counselor as gatekeeper: Social interaction in interviews*. New York, NY: Academic Press.

Fiksdal, S. (1990). *The right time and pace: A microanalysis of cross-cultural gatekeeping interviews*. Norwood, NJ: Ablex.

Fiksdal, S. (2001). "Voices in seminar: Ideologies and identities." In B. L. Smith & J. McCann (Eds.). *Reinventing ourselves: Interdisciplinary education, collaborative learning, and experimentation in higher education* (pp. 179–194), Boston, MA: Anker.

Fiksdal, S. (2008). "Metaphorically speaking: Gender and classroom discourse." In R. Dirven & G. Kristiansen (Eds.), *Cognitive sociolinguistics: Language variation, cultural models, social systems* (pp. 419–448). Berlin: Mouton de Gruyters.

Finkel, D. L. (2000). *Teaching with our mouth shut*. Portsmouth, NH: Heinemann.

Foucault, M. (1972). *The archeology of knowledge and the discourse on language*. (S. S. Smith, Trans.). New York, NY: Harper.

Gabelnick, F. MacGregor, J. Matthews, R. S. & Smith, B. L. (1990) Learning communities: Creating connections among students, faculty and disciplines. *New Directions for Teaching and Learning*, *41*. San Francisco, Jossey-Bass.

Gee, J. P. (2011). *An introduction to discourse analysis: Theory and method* (3rd ed.). New York, NY & London: Routledge.

Gibson, W., Hall, A., & Callery, P. (2006). "Topicality and the structure of interactive talk in face-to-face seminar discussions: Implications for research in distributed learning media." *British Educational Research Journal*, *32*, 77–94.

Goffman, E. (1967). *Interaction ritual: Essays in face-to-face behavior*. New York, NY: Pantheon Books.

Hafner, J. W., Sturgell, J. L., Matlock, D. L., Bockewitz, E. G., & Barker, L. T. (2012). "'Stayin' alive': A novel mental metronome to maintain compression rates in simulated cardiac arrests. *The Journal of Emergency Medicine*, *43*, e373–e377.

Henson, J., & Denker, K. (2007, Nov 1). "I'm a republican but please don't tell: An application of spirals of silence theory to classroom climate." *Conference Papers: National Communication Association*, 1–24.

Herring, S. C. (2003). "Gender and power in on-line communication." In J. Holmes & M. Meyerhoff (Eds.). *The handbook of language and gender* (pp. 202–228). Malden, MA: Blackwell.

Hintz, D. M. (2007). "Past tense forms and their functions in South Conchucos Quechua: Time, evidentiality, discourse structure, and affect." Ph.D. dissertation. University of California, Santa Barbara.

Holland, D., & Quinn, N. (Eds.). (1987). *Cultural models in language and thought*. Cambridge: Cambridge University Press.

Holmes, J. (1995). *Women, men and politeness*. London & New York, NY: Longman.

Jaffe, J., Beebe, B., Feldstein, S., Crown, C. L., Jasnow, M. D., Rochat, P., & Stern, D. N. (2001). "Rhythms of dialogue in infancy: Coordinated timing in development." *Monographs of the Society for Research in Child Development*, *66*(2), 1–149.

Johnson, A. G. (2006). *Privilege, power, and difference* (2nd ed.). Boston, MA: McGraw Hill.

Johnstone, B. (2002). *Discourse analysis*. Malden, MA: Blackwell.

Kliewer, J. R. (2001). "The innovative colleges and universities of the 1960s and 1970s: Lessons from six alternative institutions." In B. L. Smith & J. McCann (Eds.). *Reinventing ourselves: Interdisciplinary education, collaborative learning, and experimentation in higher education* (pp. 19–49). Boston, MA: Anker.

Kramarae, C., & Treichler, P. A. (1990). "Power relationships in the classroom." In S. L. Gabriel, & I. Smithson (Eds.). *Gender in the classroom: Power and pedagogy* (pp. 41–59). Champaign, IL: University of Illinois Press.

Kruse, O. (2006). "The origin of writing in the disciplines: Traditions of seminar writing and the Humboldtian ideal of the research university." *Written Communication*, *23*, 331–352.

Labov, W. (1972). *Sociolinguistic patterns*. Philadelphia, PA: University of Pennsylvania Press.

Labov, W. (1981). *The study of nonstandard English*. Urbana, IL: National Council of Teachers of English

Lakoff, G., & Johnson, M. (1980). *Metaphors we live by*. Chicago, IL: University of Chicago Press.

Lalli, C. B., & Feger, S. (2005). *Gauging and improving interactions in online seminars for mathematics coaches*. Providence, RI: Brown University. Available at: www.alliance. brown.edu (accessed May 2012).

Lapadat, J. C. (2007). "Discourse devices used to establish community, increase coherence, and negotiate agreement in an online university course." *Journal of Distance Education (Revue de L'Education à Distance)*, 21, 59–92.

Laufgraben, J. L., & Shapiro, N. S. (2004). *Sustaining and improving learning communities*. San Francisco, CA: Jossey-Bass.

Lave, J., & Wenger, E. (1991). *Situated learning: Legitimated peripheral participation*. Cambridge: Cambridge University Press.

Leap, W. L. (1999). "Language, socialization, and silence in gay adolescence." In M. Bucholtz, A. C. L., & L.A. Sutton (Eds.). *Reinventing identities: The gendered self in discourse* (pp. 95–106). New York, NY: Oxford University Press.

Lester, J. N., & Paulus, T. M. (2011). "Accountability and public displays of knowing in an undergraduate computer-mediated communication context." *Discourse Studies*, 13, 671–686.

McCann, J. (2001). "Students on interdisciplinary education: How they learn and what they learn." In B. L. Smith & J. McCann (Eds.). *Reinventing ourselves: Interdisciplinary education, collaborative learning, and experimentation in higher education* (pp. 355–367). Boston, MA: Anker.

Marshall, L., & Rowland, F. (2013). *A guide to learning independently* (5th ed.). Sydney, Australia: Pearson.

Mino, J. (2013). "Link aloud: Making interdisciplinary learning visible and audible." *Learning Communities Research and Practice*, 1(1), Article 4. Available at: http:// washingtoncenter.evergreen.edu/lcrpjournal/vol1/iss1/4 (retrieved Oct 2013).

Morgan, M. (2010). "The presentation of indirectness and power in everyday life." *Journal of Pragmatics*, 42, 283–291.

Morrish, E. (2002). "The case of the indefinite pronoun: Discourse and the concealment of lesbian identity in class." In L. Litosseliti & J. Sunderland (Eds.). *Gender identity and discourse analysis* (pp. 177–192). Amsterdam and Philadelphia, PA: John Benjamins.

Nakane, I. (2006). "Silence and politeness in intercultural communication in university seminars." *Journal of Pragmatics*, 38, 1811–1835.

Ong, W. J. (1981). *Fighting for life: Contest, sexuality, and consciousness*. Ithaca, NY: Cornell University Press.

Pavlenko, A. (2005). *Emotions and multilingualism*. New York, NY: Cambridge University Press

Portman, J., Bui, T. T., Ogaz, J., & Treviño, J. (2009). Available at: https://portfolio. du.edu/portfolio/getportfoliofile?uid=148580 (accessed August 2013).

Reddy, M. J. (1979). "The conduit metaphor: A case of frame conflict in our language about language." In A. Ortony (Ed.). *Metaphor and thought* (pp. 284–324). New York, NY: Cambridge University Press.

Reed, B. S. (2010). "Speech rhythm across turn transitions in cross-cultural talk-in-interaction." *Journal of Pragmatics*, *42*, 1037–1059.

Rees-Miller, J. (2000). "Power, severity, and context in disagreement." *Journal of Pragmatics*, *32*, 1087–1111.

Reisman, K. (1974). "Contrapuntal conversations in an Antiguan village." In R. Bauman & J. Sherzer (Eds.). *Explorations in the Ethnography of Speaking* (pp. 110–124). Cambridge: Cambridge University Press.

Schleef, E. (2008). "Gender and academic discourse: Global restrictions and local possibilities." *Language in Society*, *37*, 515–538.

Scollon, R., & Scollon, S. (1981). *Narrative, literacy and face in interethnic communication*. Norwood, NJ: Ablex.

Sensoy, Ö., & DiAngelo, R. (2012). *Is everybody equal?: An introduction to key concepts in social justice education*. New York, NY: Teachers College Press.

Sinclair, J. McH., & Coulthard, M. (1975). *Towards an analysis of discourse*. London: Oxford University Press.

Sobieraj, S., & Berry, J. M. (2011). "From incivility to outrage: Political discourse in blogs, talk radio, and cable news." *Political Communication*, *28*, 19–41.

Sue, D. W. (2010). *Microaggressions in everyday life: Race, gender, and sexual orientation*. Hoboken, NJ: Wiley.

Sue, D. W., Capodilupo, C. M., Torino, G. C., Bucceri, J. M., Holder, A. M., Nadal, K. L., & Esquilin, M. E. (2007). "Racial microaggressions in everyday life: Implications for counseling." *The American Psychologist*, *62*, 271–286.

Tagliamonte, S. (2005). "So who? Like how? Just what? Discourse markers in the conversation of young Canadians." *Journal of Pragmatics*, *37*, 1896–1915.

Tannen, D. (1981). "New York Jewish conversational style." *International Journal of the Sociology of Language*, *30*, 133–149.

Tannen, D. (1990). "You just don't understand: Women and men in conversation." New York, NY: William Morrow.

Tatum, B. D. (2003). *"Why are all the black kids sitting together in the cafeteria?"* (3rd ed.). New York, NY: Basic Books.

Tomason, W. R., & Hopper, R. (1992). "Pauses, transition relevance, and speaker change." *Human Communication Research*, *18*(3), 429–444.

Turino, T. (2008). *Music as social life: The politics of participation*. Chicago, IL: University of Chicago Press.

Uhmann, S. (1992). "Contextualizing relevance: On some forms and functions of speech rate changes in everyday conversation." In P. Auer & A. Di Luzio (Eds.), *The contextualization of language* (pp. 297–336). Amsterdam: John Benjamins.

Watts, R. J. (2003). *Politeness*. Cambridge: Cambridge University Press.

White, J. W. (2011). "Resistance to classroom participation: Minority students, academic discourse, cultural conflicts, and issues of representation in whole class discussions." *Journal of Language, Identity, and Education*, *10*, 250–265. doi: 10.1080/ 15348458.2011.598128

Wise, A. F., Perera, N., Hsiao, Y.-T., Speer, J., & Marbouti, F. (2012). "Microanalytic case studies of individual participation patterns in an asynchronous online discussion in an undergraduate blended course." *Internet and Higher Education*, *15*, 108–117. doi:10.1016/j.iheduc.2011.11.007

Wolfe, J. (2000). "Gender, ethnicity, and classroom discourse: Communication patterns of Hispanic and White students in networked classrooms." *Written Communication*, *17*, 491–519.

Yuasa, I. P. (2010). "Creaky voice: A new feminine voice quality for young urban-oriented upwardly mobile American women?" *American Speech*, *85*, 315–337.

# Index